147 Practical Tips for Emerging Scholars

From Publishing to Time Management, Grant Seeking, and Beyond

By Kathleen P. King & Ann Cranston-Gingras

Atwood Publishing
Madison, WI

147 Practical Tips for Emerging Scholars: From Publishing to Time Management, Grant Seeking, and Beyond
By Kathleen P. King & Ann Cranston-Gingras

www.atwoodpublishing.com

ISBN 978-1-891859-89-2

Printed in the United States of America.

Cover design by Tamara Dever, TLC Graphics, www.tlcgraphics.com

Library of Congress Cataloging-in-Publication Data

King, Kathleen P., 1958-
147 tips for emerging scholars : from publishing to time management, grant seeking, and beyond / Kathleen P. King & Ann Cranston-Gingras, University of South Florida.
pages cm
Includes bibliographical references and index.
ISBN 978-1-891859-89-2 (alk. paper)
1. College teachers—Vocational guidance—United States. 2. Scholars—Vocational guidance—United States. 3. Learning and scholarship—United States. I. Cranston-Gingras, Ann. II. Title. III. Title: One hundred and forty-seven tips for emerging scholars. IV. Title: One hundred forty-seven tips for emerging scholars.
LB1778.2.K55 2014
378.1'2023—dc23

2014004291

Dedication

We dedicate this volume to two groups of people within higher education: 1) those mentors who shaped our minds, hearts, and actions, and 2) those students and colleagues with whom we walk the same journey as mentor and guide.

Our vision of the professional academic life and mentoring usually is largely influenced by our teachers and professors. In this vein, Kathy dedicates this book to two women professors at Widener University who helped shape her vision of empowerment, initiative, and creativity as academics: Drs. Patricia A. Lawler and Antonia D'Onofrio. She also remembers those mentor colleagues who invested their efforts in her pretenure journey at Fordham University: Drs. Rowland Hughes, Angela Carrisquillo, Terry Cicchelli, Joanna Uhry, and John Houtz.

Ann recognizes the influence of the many doctoral students she has mentored to graduation and dedicates this book to them. Several of these were students who faced significant health challenges along the way. Others managed intense work and family responsibilities while completing their programs. The success of each of these students is a testament to the power of persistence in the face of obstacles.

Acknowledgments

We recognize and appreciate the valuable contributions of several doctoral students and graduates who reviewed this book's draft manuscript. They enthusiastically provided encouraging feedback and direction for us. In this capacity, we specifically thank Dr. Carol Burg, Karen Eggeling, Susan Henzel-Speer, Rebecca Puig, Christina Partin, and Katie Lyman.

Table of Contents

Introduction

147 Tips for Emerging Scholars assists you in developing your successful professional journey as a scholar by delivering proven and succinct guidance. It builds on your prior experiences to create greater opportunities. Rather than hoping for good luck or fortune, piecing together stray bits of information, or risking trusting the wrong people, you can use this book as a ready reference that you can turn to again and again for solid direction, clarity, and encouragement.

The central question we address in this book is this: How does one succeed in developing a career as a scholar? In answering this question, we provide direction about the more detailed and necessary concerns that compose the bigger picture. For instance, what areas do scholars need to address while developing their careers? How can emerging scholars find information and support for each of these areas? What are suggestions for organizing, or tracking these efforts in order to increase efficiency, motivation, and required documentation? What and where are the most frequent roadblocks and obstacles encountered? How can such obstacles be avoided or overcome?

Reading the sample questions our book addresses doubtless reminds many readers that not all academic programs prepare doctoral students for success in these areas. Various academic programs may focus on some of these areas, while others may not address life beyond graduation at all: and that is exactly why we daily find faculty seeking support in so many ways.

Unfortunately, many faculty never find enough effective support within their existing network. They are not able to find suitable supportive colleagues among campus-based mentors, or off-campus colleagues, academics, or even prior professors. This difficult and frustrating situation is another reason we wrote this book. We provide strategic tips to "fill the gap" and guide you in creating your unique pathway to being a scholar in your discipline whether you have a current support team of 100, 10, 1, or none.

Who Can Benefit from this Book?

We designed this book with your specific needs in mind. This section discusses the book's broad appeal across audiences, including doctoral students preparing for faculty careers, new professors, and mid-career or advanced faculty. We believe the ideas and strategies will benefit all faculty by providing fresh perspectives about designing research agendas and projects, pursuing publishing opportunities, writing grants, and developing overall greater efficiency in their ongoing career development. We particularly recognize the needs of doctoral students and new faculty because the stakes are high and time is short to meet their goals.

Doctoral Students

As we have worked with doctoral students over many years and used many of these recommendations along the way, we have seen large and small benefits. It makes a big difference when scholars know what lies ahead and how they need to progress for a successful career. Using the doctoral study years to begin building a strong research and publishing record, gaining experience in teaching, and developing a professional network is invaluable in not only immediate results (finishing your degree), but also securing your first position.

It is exciting to learn how these strategies help students immediately in their journey as scholars and provide a strong foundation on which to develop a successful academic career, as described by Boyer (1997) and others: a vital research agenda, lifelong productivity, and professional confidence. Considering that the alternative to success is to flounder, spin your wheels, and potentially lose key employment and career opportunities, these results are essential knowledge and practice for faculty careers.

We know that it is unlikely you will fully comprehend and appreciate everything you read in this book the first time. It's a lot to digest. Instead, we suggest that you consult the book as needed and gradually work through it prior to graduating or interviewing for your first position. This strategy will provide an overview to frame your understanding of academic life, as well as alert you to sections you may need to access as needs arise.

New Faculty

For new faculty, teaching preparations, tenure and promotion requirements, and meeting scores of faculty, staff, and students, are just a few of the critical things that will dominate your first 9-12 months after hire. In the midst of such a steep learning curve, this book offers strategies for developing efficient approaches and determining critical priorities.

In addition to the specific decisions facing new faculty, there are the many challenges all faculty encounter, with a multitude of competing demands and opportunities arising each day and week. In the midst of this exhilarating environment are the pressures to be self-disciplined in reaching your most important goal: building a strong record which qualifies you for tenure and promotion.

This book will guide you through the webs of understanding higher education structures, dynamics, and governance. It will also provide strategies for building your research and publishing record efficiently. Moreover, we embed key tips for surviving in the academy—from teaching and networking to grant writing and beyond. Please remember that you may not comprehend everything the first time you read this book. Instead, become acquainted with the contents you need immediately, explore the others, and then refer back to sections as needed. We hope the book validates your choices when you are on the right track, and prompts you to both move ahead and persevere to the next stage of faculty life.

Experienced Faculty

For an experienced faculty member, this book can provide suggestions for new dimensions of development. Exploring opportunities for publishing, grant writing, and mentoring may open new approaches or avenues, which can be richly rewarding. In addition, you may review this book with a dual focus, not only for yourself, but also for guidance in how to mentor colleagues and students.

Over the years, we may build strong professional networks, but remain narrowly focused in our fields. Consulting a book such as this one can introduce different perspectives from the ones customarily considered. One of the many reasons the academy is exciting for faculty is that we can pursue many different areas of responsibility during our careers. Our major focus may be teaching, research, publishing, or grant administration at different times with the option to focus on the ones we enjoy the best, or within which we currently have the best opportunities. Our intention with the strategies and perspective provided in this volume is to provide keen insight and strategies for all these areas, thereby illuminating more opportunities and expediting your success.

Overview of the Book

In order to address academics needs, *147 Tips for Emerging Scholars* has three major sections. First is the introductory material, including this Preface and Chapters 1 and 2. These foundational chapters introduce the unique audiences, structure, and ways to use this volume for maximum benefit. The chapters also provide an overview of the authors' orientation to succeeding in the academic life—fundamental strategies that frame most of our efforts. The second section is the major body of this work: the 147 tips. The tips are divided into 11 categories grouped by topic. These divisions help orient the reader to the topic at hand, and also provide ease of reference later. The end materials comprise the third section of the book and include the appendices, references, etc. We spent much time assembling these resources, as we know that during our own journeys we often sought such materials. We address this need with a rich selection of reading materials, references, and charts—both in these end materials and throughout the book.

Many concepts and issues introduced in this book may be new to early-career academics; therefore, we used several means to communicate the meaning and specifics most fully. Across the volume we use graphics, concept maps, figures, and tables to illustrate principles and enumerate examples or details. In addition, we provide sample worksheets, charts, and templates that were helpful to us and our mentees. Most of these we developed ourselves, and in a few cases we borrowed them with permission.

Kathleen P. King
Ann Cranston-Gingras
University South Florida
Tampa, FL

CHAPTER 1:

Time Management and the Missing Operating Instructions

A Frequent Equation: Too Many Demands, and Too Little Direction

Dr. Sheila Graves graduated from a prestigious research university with her PhD in sociology four years ago. She had landed a tenure track position right after her dissertation defense and relocated that summer. She found it no surprise that her position included an enormous multitude of demands for research, publication, teaching, and service. However, she was not prepared for the complexities of coping with the competing demands and deadlines, demystifying the peer review publication pathway, and deciphering expectations from the many stakeholders involved in deciding her future.

The biggest problem was that she was at the fourth-year tenure review point and the tenure and promotion committee had made it clear that her progress was not on target. They pointed out her shortcomings, and with great emphasis and clarity described the consequences of not addressing them. However, they did not discuss how she could navigate a successful course over the next two years.

Sheila was already exhausted from the many stresses, long nights, and demands of these first few years. She did not know where to turn, whom to trust, or where to start. She knew she wanted to succeed, but she felt as though she was continuing to spin her wheels. She bemusedly thought this was one instance when she would be glad to read operating instructions.

Support for the Academic's Journey

You may be either a doctoral student or have recently earned your doctorate, and while you may have gained some direction for your professional career, you still find you have unanswered questions. In the case above, it is obvious that Dr. Graves did not have clear direction to plan and advance her career as a scholar. This is unfortunately quite common. In retrospect, very few of us ever did.

Instead, we spent our years as emerging scholars determining how to handle successfully a myriad of responsibilities and unknown factors. If we were fortunate, our doctoral studies prepared us for this at least to some degree. Alternatively, we found an experienced colleague who was willing to walk besides us on the journey. However, even with these aids, we still had to figure out a great deal of the journey ourselves. Why? Because both the situations and conditions we found ourselves in were unique. Moreover, every faculty member has a unique blend of talents, skills, needs, and desires with which to cope, leverage, and develop during their journey. These variable assets mean none of us travels the same pathway in our development as an academic and scholar. However, our experience reveals that there are many meaningful common threads and supports available.

This book addresses the unique issues and opportunities facing faculty who seek to chart a successful career in higher education. Based on where you are in your faculty career, and on your future goals, you may have different needs for this book. However, we have some overall suggestions regarding how to use it for your professional advancement and continued learning.

How to Use this Book

Often higher education faculty do not have excessive direct supervision. Specifically, we do not customarily have daily or weekly performance oversight. Instead, administrators and colleagues expect us to be self-directed in planning and evaluating most of our time and effort (Fink 2003). Therefore, in order to ensure success, it is necessary that we independently develop strategies for goal-setting, project management, and self-direction. By using this book, you will be learning some of these skills, which you can then put into practice in your specific field and context. You have a great opportunity with this book. You can operationalize what you learn, or you can let it pass by. Which will be your choice?

R-Plan: Making this Book Work for You

R-Plan is the brief name we devised for the plan which guides our readers to gain the most from this book. The "R" stands for three major elements in the strategy: Review, Reflect, and Revise. In addition, "Plan" is the core message of our book. Rather than floating down the wild river and torrents of academic life without a map or a paddle, we believe in informed planning. This section briefly explains the R-Plan strategy.

As you can see immediately below, the R-Plan's complete name is "R-Plan to Enjoy the Journey." This name communicates the overall emphasis of our philosophy about faculty careers. We believe that faculty can enjoy the many opportunities and phases embedded in their careers if they have the essential information and if they use it to plan for success.

R-Plan to Enjoy the Journey:

- Review and Reflect
- Work Your Plan
- Reflect on the Challenges
- Continue to Network
- Rejoice for the Success
- Revise and Implement
- Enjoy the Journey!

This brief discussion of the R-Plan elements reveals our belief that faculty need to be proactive in both developing their plan and enjoying it! We believe faculty need to use the information we share to determine their goals and then take action to reach them. By introducing this approach up front in our book, we hope readers will be better equipped to understand our reasoning and thereby advance their faculty careers. We know faculty want their intellectual curiosity satisfied. We respect and value those precious traits; therefore, we share the plan.

Review and Reflect

Reflective practice is foundational to higher education faculty progressing in their careers. As stated prior, faculty do not have a direct supervisor or manager who oversees their daily performance or "production." In fact, such direct management would cause severe conflict in higher education culture in the United States and faculty would not tolerate it (Fink 2003; Schrecker 2010). Therefore, those faculty who succeed in the USA's system must independently understand and pursue the requirements and expectations for success. Faculty cannot expect the higher education institution to provide complete guidance and mentoring in this matter. We are not traditional "work for hire" personnel (Fink 2003). Instead, in some ways, faculty are more akin to independent contractors who have a long-term continuing relationship with an institution. Consider the following: colleges and universities do not own the intellectual property we create as part of our salaried work; we generally do not punch a clock, nor maintain timesheets; we work primarily independently, or in collaboration with others of our choosing, in delivering the services we have been hired to perform.

However, when we think about our activities and agendas from this fresh perspective, new observations and opportunities may arise. For instance, how do I determine how much is enough time for preparing class, correcting student work, conducting research, etc.? If I do not have to punch a clock, what options do I have regarding structuring my work week?

As these questions illustrate, examining expectations, meanings, and definitions at a level deeper than face value stimulates examining unquestioned assumptions. In order to assist our readers in implementing the strategies and approaches we suggest, we include reflection and personal activities along with the tips. In these ways, this book supports reflection, with the details that stalls many efforts. By establishing a modifiable plan, faculty step beyond inertia. Now, they are in motion, and it becomes a matter of directing their energies to the most productive and worthwhile ends each day. We refer to this stage as "working the plan."

Work Your Plan

For example, each day as Kathy reviews her electronic calendar, she sees not only meetings, office hours, planning class, delivering classes, and sundry appointments, but also small and large blocks of time reserved for research and writing activities. Students and faculty gasp when they see her calendar the first time, but these folks are also puzzled by her writing productivity. Kathy says, "From my perspective, I create appointments 'with myself' to do the essential work of my career. Many colleagues find this to be another of my odd organizational habits. However, it is my norm; I wonder why other people don't do the same."

Consider the way faculty customarily pursue their time and responsibilities. Most people will identify appointments, office hours, and classes in their paper or electronic schedule. The way our weeks transpire, faculty report to the office at least several days a week. And aside from professors who spend large amounts of times in laboratories, when we are not teaching our campus time is mostly dominated by phone calls, email correspondence, and students and colleagues arriving at our office door for pre-arranged or spontaneous meetings/visits. Some of our on-campus time is spent traveling across campus and participating in college or university meetings. All of this work is valid and important and represents different roles and responsibilities of our careers.

However, how many of you, like us, arrive on campus with a pre-planned day and walk out the door 8-12 hours later with the day being a blur? Instead of the 5-10 items which were supposed to be accomplished, 20-30 took their place, and only 3-4 on the original list may have been conquered. The day is a blur, time flies, and you eat your lunch at your desk while listening to voicemail. Instead of accomplishment, exhaustion overruns you—emotionally and mentally.

In these circumstances, who controls the plan and agenda of your days, weeks, and career? Happenstance, immediate crises, urgency, and "administrivia" no doubt control 60-70% of it.

UNLESS, we work our plan.

In the section above, we established a plan. Next we need to review the plan daily, determine which needs are the most urgent to address, and accomplish the critical elements of our work agenda. These are decisions and choices we must commit to daily.

We need to stand against the tyranny of the urgent and adopt a new strategy which no longer allows circumstances to rule. Faculty are generally very bright people. We are capable of regaining control of our time, focus, and energy, especially when it increases our professional productivity and growth. In order to do so, we also need to limit the time, energy, and attention which we allow nonessential activities to consume. But how exactly can we make this happen in a climate where urgency seems to drive everyone and everything? The secret is to plan our steps and work our plan.

Returning to Kathy's weekly planning routine as an example, she shares her major strategies she consistently employs:

1. First, I identify several small and large blocks in my calendar and make appointments 'with myself' or my writing partners for writing and publication.

2. Second, since these writing times include the days I select to work off-campus, I then consolidate my on-campus work. I know I teach on campus "x" number of days per week; therefore, I designate office hours for several hours prior to class on the same days. By consolidating office hours and classes, I have more off-campus time to write and less distraction from the tyranny of the urgent during those times.

3. Third, I determine my own time limit to complete all administrative details, non-urgent requests, and emails (otherwise fondly known as "maintenance"). This strategy can overcome the common experience of such details expanding to all available time. How do I control this time? Based on the needs of the day and week, I assign the number of minutes needed for such details (30, 60, 75, 90, etc). Then I set two phone or computer alarms: one fifteen minutes prior to the end of the time I have allotted, and the other at the end of the time. This helps me rein in this "maintenance" work so that it does not expand further. Because my major assignment has not been administration, my goal is to maintain a firm time limit and not become sidelined or "sucked into" allowing these activities to dominate my day.

4. Obviously, if I need an extra few minutes, I allow for it. However, if I need an extra 30 minutes, either my judgment of time and effort is incorrect or I am spending too much time on each task, perhaps sidelined by other trivia or nonessentials. (No, this does not only happen to you; we all fight this battle.)

5. Another successful strategy is to limit the time you check and respond to email and phone calls. For instance, Kathy checks four times a day, which keeps the response list shorter: morning, mid-day, afternoon, and late evening. She allocates 30–60 minutes for the bulk of correspondence in the morning, and a

maximum of 15, 15, and 5 minutes, respectively, for midday, afternoon, and late-evening checks.

Looking at this approach across an entire day, it means that you focus more attention on writing and research instead of phone calls, email, or social media dominating every minute of the day. Recent data reveal the reason this approach is essential for our productivity.

Researchers have discovered that while we currently frequently multitask many activities in our work and private lives, we actually allocate less attention and focus on any one of those areas when multitasking than when single-minded (Hamilton 2008; Rubinstein, Meyer, and Evans 2001). The result is that when I postpone phone calls, email, and social media, shut the door or work away from my office, I can produce 3,000 words of good text in half a day. The alternative scenario, dividing my attention across competing demands, results in consuming 12–36 hrs to accomplish the same outcome. Wouldn't you rather make a conscious choice about how to spend those additional 12–36 hours, rather than letting it slip through the hourglass? I think of how I might invest those hours for several valuable purposes: advancing the current project, commencing or completing another project, physical exercise, recreation, family, or refreshment! Isn't that realization a powerful motivation to work the plan? In fact, it leads us to the first of our "Reflect on the Challenges" phase.

Reflect on the Challenges

The next stage in our productivity model may be unexpected; however, we find it is an invaluable investment in fine-tuning our plan and reaching our goals efficiently. This "Reflect on the Challenges" phase explicitly provides time to pause and consider what may be delaying or blocking our progress. By building this stage into the process, either we develop a habit of mind to consider the challenges before they become insurmountable, or we spin our wheels unsuccessfully for too long.

Specifically, the challenges we refer to may include obstacles, barriers, unknown variables, or uncertainties we encounter as we implement our scholarly plan. We suggest reflecting on the plan you established, your progress, and asking, "Is anything delaying my progress?" If so, identify what those issues or concerns are and develop a plan to overcome them.

In some cases, you might need to identify workshops for specialized training (for new research or analysis techniques, or more advanced writing skills). In other situations, you might need additional information from the institution or colleagues (for example on how to gain cooperation from an office or recruit more research participants). A fruitful tactic is to discuss the situation with knowledgeable colleagues; they are usually quite willing to support academic growth and it provides an opportunity for you to gain professional feedback and encouragement on your research.

In our experience of developing our scholarly research and writing, very few challenges remain insurmountable when addressed with a willingness to continue to learn, determination to work, colleagues' insight and support, and persistence. In addition, these challenges also cultivate greater commitment to our goals, and increase the ultimate pleasure in reaching them.

Continue to Network

Many people, both within and beyond the academy, think that faculty complete most of their work in isolation from others. Instead, however, we spend a great deal of time in meetings, with students, and at conferences. This pattern is a result of governance structure, our teaching and publication roles, and available vehicles for professional development. However, we may leverage these encounters further to build greater productivity and knowledge for us as scholars. There are at least two major purposes that make continuing to network through these different avenues vital for the emerging scholar: new opportunities and formative direction.

When you engage in these events with an open mind, eager to discover what other people beyond and within your discipline have discovered, you likely will experience what Kathy does: that "new opportunities sprout quicker than weeds in a springtime lawn." Such opportunities may include participating in research, grants, or writing papers, but may also be the emergence of concepts, ideas, and learning. Specifically, while we might grow a great deal personally and professionally when engaged in community, the opportunities for new connections in our thinking, the juxtaposition of similar and dissimilar content and concepts, cultivate unique triggers and environments for novel ideas to synergize and grow. For instance, the frequent situation of explaining our specialized research to someone outside of our discipline can force us to use different vocabulary, and therefore step outside of our tired jargon. In order to help others understand, we may need different examples to connect their experience to the concepts familiar to us. For us, a critical benefit of this dialogue includes thinking about our work, writing project, or problem from a different vantage point. Often such different perspectives can reveal strengths, weaknesses, and new solutions hidden previously in the shadows.

The other critical benefit which many faculty do not realize they gain from dialogue with colleagues is formative direction. Again, considering that when we discuss our research or writing with someone regardless of their position to our discipline, their questions and insights may provide new information or insights. In addition, even if their view does not fit exactly, the process of questioning leads us to develop deeper understandings, ask more questions, follow different paths, explore additional resources, have more discussions, and gather more data. We choose to name this constellation of experiences "formative development."

Returning to our previous automotive analogy, while our "research vehicle" moves, we can interpret how these conversations reveal possible shortcuts, detours, or alternate routes. Such redirection may afford savings in time or money, new sights to see (new observations), or travel companions (collaborators). The collaborative conversations or relationships can guide us to change the process, writing plan, or research while in progress and thereby inform our efforts. If we remain in isolation, we miss the opportunity for feedback as our ideas and work develop. In such cases, we miss catching pitfalls before they emerge, or recognizing a storm on the horizon. Formative development is a powerful result of meaningful collegial dialogue and reveals one essential role of professional networking.

Enjoy the Journey!

For two major purposes, we have found that faculty must invest themselves in cultivating their personal growth and refreshment by Enjoying the Journey. We will call these purposes the Two E's: Efficiency and Effervescence.

Efficiency represents the fact that when we invest time in recreation and refreshment, our creativity and productivity increases. How many times have you been log-jammed trying to solve a problem or find the best ways to write that article and have been completely unable to find the right solution? Do you ever walk away and "discover" the answer while doing something different entirely?

Kathy remembers when she was writing one of her first books back in northern New Jersey: "I had a new house and made a plan to gradually purchase and plant flowers and hedges over the next few weekends. It was summer and I was only teaching one class, so per my usual schedule, I was mostly working at my home office, plugging away twelve hours a day writing, analyzing data, and writing some more. In addition, as much as I love writing, I wrote this free verse to describe the happiest moments that summer:

> Stark moments of inspiration and insight…
> Times where new turns of phrases or conceptual models dawned on me…
> Happened
> Not
> At the computer keyboard
> But with dirt under my fingernails and a trowel in my hand.

Digging in the earth and pressing soil around fragile flower roots required a form of concentration and activity that provided insight and fresh energy for the writing project upstairs in my home office. Far separated from both the physical space and activity flow of the writing process is where many of Kathy's insights mentally coalesce. Ann has had similar experiences while working out in the gym. Later in the volume, we will mention this topic, as there is an entire literature regarding the connections between mindfulness and writing (Goldberg 2005; Moore 2012).

Effervescence: A similar lesson emerges from the dilemma illustrated in the next all too frequent scenario:

> It is late at night, when this nocturnal professor is wont to be blasting out page after page of text. The clock scurries at high speed towards 1 am and the dogs whimper to go to bed. Yet at these times, the urgency and desperation grow from the feeling that the ideas burn within me and threaten to disappear forever if I stop. However, I know from the past that if I fight against this panic and pursue the rest I need, when I resume the next morning I will have more ideas and better direction. To safeguard against losing my flow of my writing and composition, I jot down bullet points of my thoughts.

In fact, this is a frequent scenario for Kathy and those few notes she jots down at 1 am jumpstart her train of thought the next day. Indeed, she finds that her productivity drastically increases when she wakes up with renewed effervescence and a fresh mind, eyes, and heart.

(Note to self: Read this section the next time The Late Night Writing Tyranny seeks to control you!)

Revise and Implement

The Revise and Implement phase of the model emphasizes that faculty are in the knowledge field; therefore we need to be lifelong learners. This need is stronger than ever, with the rapid changes happening in society, politics, economics, and new technology constantly emerging (Tapscott 2008). The opportunities to pursue our research, reflect, network, and thereby expand our perspectives lay the groundwork for the continuing revisions and implementations needed in our plan.

Another emphasis of this phase is for ongoing learning, growth, and development. In Kathy's book (2009), *The Handbook of the Evolving Research of Transformative Learning*, she describes how her understanding of research and transformative learning changed after completing her doctorate and experienced the next ten years researching the topic. Examples of such growth and development include growing in discipline-specific knowledge and/or practice, cultivating additional skills, and scaffolding thinking to new structures/perspectives. In turn, we incorporate our changing understanding and perspectives in our research, realize that it is dynamic, and pursue new offshoots of opportunities, improvement, and implementation. If we return to our metaphor, emerging scholars must continue to explore new directions and chart new courses.

Rejoice in the Successes

The "Rejoice in the Successes" phase represents the essential reflecting, questioning, and refreshment processes for the development of well-balanced and authentic scholars and teachers (Miller 1994; O'Reilley 1998). The rejoicing we describe consists of two essential elements: celebration and authenticity.

Even as we dedicate ourselves to work hard in planning, implementing, and following through to success in our work of research, writing, publishing, and teaching, we must also celebrate the successes we achieve. Whether it is our first journal article or our 50th, first book or 10th, a college award or professional research award, the moments are not frequent, so we do well to enjoy them when they arrive. Such celebration is also time to consider the path to the goal. We can reflect on what worked well, what didn't, and how to overcome similar challenges next time. We also want to consider thanking people who have been supportive of our work: family, friends, colleagues, funders. This is a time to share the wealth of the good news and enlist more people to be invested in your future. Surely, the academic life can be isolating at times, but if we welcome others into our success, we will guard against that risk.

In this context of coping with faculty life, many authors, including Cranton (2001), Apps (1991), Palmer (1999), Miller (1994), and others, also discuss the need for *authenticity* among faculty. As defined by several sources, we experience authenticity when our public and private selves are consistent. Whenever we seek to "construct" a persona or "play a part" in our professional and personal relationships, we drift from the powerful, grounding benefits of authenticity. The fact is that part of our teaching emanates from our development as individuals and scholars, because our lives and work fundamentally integrate this characteristic. Moreover, successful, healthy, and productive faculty relationships, mentoring roles, and community, organizational and professional service are more effective and rewarding when we participate authentically.

A helpful way to consider how to build authenticity is to cultivate our focus on being and becoming comfortable and happy with our strengths and weaknesses, and reaching towards self actualization (Miller 1994; Moore 2012; Palmer 1999; Schön 1983). If we recognize authenticity as a valuable characteristic in faculty roles and lives, then we will not make the journey aimlessly or without personal investment. Instead, authentic faculty will be better prepared to cultivate a well-balanced, self-defined, and insightful academic experience.

Summary

As evidenced from this introductory chapter, *147 Tips for Emerging Scholars* offers much to initiate or advance your success as a scholar, and nothing to lose as you invest a short time to read it. As coauthors, we make every effort to incorporate much needed humor, accessibility, stories, and reasonableness into the text in order to make the reading enjoyable and even fun. Our goal is that readers will find assistance in the volume for the different seasons of their academic life.

Unfortunately, as current and emerging scholars, we do not find many opportunities to pursue professional development and explore the details of career development. Our hope is that this book will be a powerful springboard for you throughout the different stages of your career.

CHAPTER 2:

How To Approach Academic Careers Systematically

Mapping the Tenure Track

Angela is a newly hired assistant professor at a metropolitan research university. Her faculty assignment consists of teaching two classes a semester, advising students, maintaining an active research agenda, and engaging in university, professional, and community service. Before the end of her first three years at the university, Angela will undergo a "mid-tenure review." At that time, the review committees expect Angela to provide written narratives describing her philosophy, goals, and progress in the areas of teaching, research, and service and to present documentation of her accomplishments in these areas. Along the way, faculty and administrators will evaluate her work each year during "annual reviews" and by the end of her sixth year, she will undergo her final review for tenure. At that point, Angela must also support fully her record of teaching, research, and service with items and artifacts illustrating her accomplishments.

Most pre-tenure faculty will face the same system Angela encounters. Yet many seem unaware that a roadmap exists. Moreover, we find many among those who do discover the tenure-track roadmap do not effectively translate the landmarks and signposts into directions for success. This chapter provides the needed navigational assistance for our readers.

Planning for Tenure Review Success

Describing how truly effective people work, Steven Covey (2004) describes the importance of beginning with "the end in mind." This principle is especially appropriate for emerging scholars who are under a time crunch to reach milestones in the areas of teaching, research, and service, all while strategically organizing documentation of their accomplishments for job seeking, tenure, and promotion purposes. It is never too soon to begin using these strategies; doctoral students, non-tenure earning faculty, and tenure track faculty all need to put these recommendations into immediate practice in order to strategize, build, track, and document their academic careers.

A common mistake many emerging and seasoned scholars make is failing to take the time to document and reflect on their accomplishments as they occur. Documentation, along with ongoing reflection about scholarly endeavors and achievements in critical areas, is essential to development as a scholar, as well as for successful navigation through the tenure and promotion process. In this chapter we present a system that emerging scholars can use to keep track of, organize, and reflect on their accomplishments in a useful way. Too often, emerging scholars ignore this area while meeting day-to-day expectations. As a result, no documentation materializes as time passes and review deadlines draw closer relentlessly.

An initial step in organizing documentation of accomplishments and beginning to reflect on expected standards of accomplishment in teaching, research, and service is to gather and review information regarding institutional expectations and evaluation criteria. For doctoral students, this includes examining their department's "experience checklists," specifying teaching, research, and service activities that students are expected to engage in during their program; reviewing sample position announcements with required and preferred qualifications, and looking over sample mid-tenure evaluation templates from universities where they aspire to be employed.

Experience checklists typically delineate those professional experiences you engaged in while ramping up your career (see Figure 2.1). They may include teaching activities such as TA experiences, co-teaching, and teaching undergraduate courses as the instructor of record; research experiences such as author and co-authorship of journal articles, conference presentations, and grant writing experiences; and service activities such as participation on department and university committees, assistance with professional association functions, and discipline related voluntary work with schools and agencies.

PROFESSIONAL EXPERIENCE	DATE/ TITLE	DETAILS (LOCATION, ETC.)
Dissertation Success & Mentoring		
Attend two dissertation proposal defenses in your department		
Attend two dissertation defenses in your department		
Once eligible, participate on a dissertation committee		
Once eligible, co-chair a dissertation committee		
Research Agenda		
Identify your research focus/foci		
Develop a concept map to illustrate your research strands		
Develop a planning chart to track your research projects		
Professional Network & Service—Local, Regional, & Beyond		
Attend one local or regional professional conference		
Attend one national professional conference		
Present or co-present at one local or regional professional conference		
Present or co-present at one national professional conference		
Join two regional or state professional conferences		
Join two national professional conferences (bonus tip: student rates are less!)		
Identify and apply for participation in committees for which you are eligible for service at each level: department, college and institution, regional and national organizations		
Participate in planning a regional or local professional conference		

Figure 2.1 Experience checklist

Professional Experience	Date/ Title	Details (location, etc.)
Publication/Conferences		
Develop a tracking chart for your in-progress and submitted projects		
Participate as co-author on conference proposal		
Participate as co-author on research article		
Participate as co-author on a book chapter		
Author and submit a conference proposal		
Author and submit a research article		
Author and submit a book chapter		
Grant Writing and Administration		
Participate as research assistant in a funded project		
Co-author a proposal for a funded project		
Solo author a grant for a funded research		
Participate as an administrator in a funded research or other project		
Teaching Development		
Identify a mentor for your teaching responsibilities		
Identify opportunity to be a teaching assistant		
Ask a colleague to conduct a peer observation of your teaching		
Service: Local, Regional, and Beyond		
Identify and apply for participation in committees for which you are eligible for service at each level: department, college and institution, regional and national organizations		
Experiences Unique to Your Field		

Figure 2.1 Experience checklist, cont.

Pre-tenure faculty should develop an experience checklist to document all their prior professional experiences that will add to their vitae and portfolio. Even though your participation in a research grant, professional conference, or publication was as a doctoral student, you should list them in your CV. More urgently, however, pre-tenure faculty must request copies of their institution's annual review guidelines, mid-tenure and tenure review applications or templates. In addition, determine if and how you may access samples of recently successful candidates' tenure and promotion applications and portfolios.

After reviewing the templates, it's a good idea to begin by setting up a filing system with the three broad categories of teaching, research, and service as the major organizers and the specific criterion found in the templates as sub-categories. The files should be kept both in hard copy and digitally, as much as possible.

A helpful recommendation is to file your artifacts along with your thoughts about how they address the criterion. For example, if one of the ways the faculty and administration will judge your accomplishments in teaching is through student evaluations, then you should immediately begin filing hard and digital copies of the evaluations you receive at the end of each semester and writing a short reflection piece to keep with each course set. If particular student comments exemplify your teaching philosophy, you can note these as examples in your reflection. In addition, file a copy of that semester's syllabus with the records and document any different or new instructional strategies or materials you implemented. These notes will not only assist you in explaining the evaluation results, but also reveal the work you invested in teaching each course.

If another criterion is publication in high impact, peer refereed journals, then as you file each of your published articles, you should also begin including documentation of the review process and impact factors for the journals in which your articles are published, as well as a short summary of how the article fits with your research focus. The peer review information regarding the journal may be found in the journal or authors' guidelines, and you may need to access a writers' guide or bibliographic resources (such as Thomson Reuter's ScienceWatch.com for the sciences) for the journal impact and manuscript acceptance ratings.

Initially, keeping the hard copies of your files in three separate binders, one each for teaching, research, and service, works well. However, as the semesters advance, you will need to move your growing collection of materials to file boxes. We suggest lightweight but durable plastic file boxes with hanging folders and neatly printed labels.

In addition, we also recommend applying the principle of redundancy with your electronic files and records. Backup your electronic data by both saving it to a CD/DVD or USB drive and online with an Internet "cloud" service. Many institutions now provide online backup services; however, if yours does not, there are several freely available. Most reliable backup services provide a minimum or 5 GB of storage, and many include much more space. Examples of these services and websites include Google.com, Dropbox.com, Mozybackup.com, and iDrive.com.

Identify Sources of Information

Table 2.1 includes some sources of expectation and evaluation information that you will need at various phases of your career. Gathering and reviewing these sources early on will help you know what items are important to save and help you with organizing your materials in advance.

Faculty should keep all of the gathered documents in both hard copy and digital copy as much as possible in order to maximize organization and decrease potential of lost documents. You will be surprised how often you will want to refer back to the original document to verify the specific expectations and your overall direction.

Plan the Experience and Plan to Gather

Specifically, this phase refers to both planning your career experience and to gather the needed materials while you are in process of building it. Many faculty who are in the midst of assembling their tenure review dossiers will testify that nothing is more frustrating than trying to find [illegible] your work after the fact. However, the reality of our professional lives is that there is often no time to stop what we are doing at the time to label and file needed items as they cross our desk. One strategy Ann uses to overcome this dilemma is to keep a simple cardboard box on the floor under her desk. During the busy week, many items needing evaluation or review cross her desk; an announcement for one of her doctoral student dissertation defenses crosses her desk, the hard copy of one of her journal articles arrive in the mail, etc. Rather than shelving them in assigned locations, she simply puts the items in the box and moves on with her day.

Professional Status	Sources of Information Regarding Expectations and Evaluation Criteria
Doctoral students	• Program career development checklist • Faculty mid-tenure application/template • Current faculty position advertisements
Pre-tenured faculty	• Faculty mid-tenure application/template • Faculty tenure application/template • Faculty promotion application/template • Annual review guidelines
Tenured faculty	• Faculty promotion application/template • Annual review template

Table 2.1 Sources of evaluation and expectation information for academics

Since her pre-tenure days, Ann's practice has been to set aside regular time to sort through the items in the box, document them in appropriate venues such as on her electronic vita, and then file the hard copies according to category in the corresponding binders or file boxes. Depending on the phase of your career, the frequency and amount of time scheduled for this task can vary. The "box" can also serve as a holding tank for items that may not readily fit into any of the evaluation categories, but could be useful for something else later. Once you familiarize yourself with the types of documentation necessary for a successful review portfolio, deciding which items to save becomes second nature and routine.

Consider that now and for the near future, many of our documents are in electronic format, and you may never receive a hardcopy of announcements or publications. What is the most reasonable strategy to create a parallel solution to the cardboard box? Of course, a virtual electronic folder which is in both your email and backed up to your online drive will be a simple solution for you to collect and save them. Likewise, you need to remind yourself that when you sort through the cardboard box, you also open the electronic folders and sort those as well. Keeping our organizing strategies up to date with the ways we do our work is one of the challenges we will all continue to face. Therefore, continue to refine these recommendations for your specific situations and changing conditions as they appear.

Domain	Experiences	Documentation (paper and electronic as available and applicable)
Teaching	• Teaching assignment • Online, blended, and other alternative delivery teaching • Mentoring of students and junior faculty • Course development • Curriculum development • Instructional strategies development • Teaching assistantship • Adjunct teaching	• Teaching philosophy and narrative • Student evaluations • Letters of recommendation • Syllabi • Samples of teaching materials • Formative evaluation • Samples of student work (with permission) • Evidence of leadership in instructional programs • Evidence of student and junior faculty mentoring

Research and Publication	• Research assignment
	• Research assistant
	• Research coordinator
	• Co-author articles, research presentations, chapters
	• Author articles, research presentations, chapter
	• Grants
	  • Grant writing
	  • Grant participation
	  • Grant Principle Investigator (PI)
		• Letters of recommendation
		• Grant applications and related RFPs (request for proposals)
		• Grant project reports
		• Grant reviews
		• Submitted manuscripts and cover letters (if not yet accepted)
		• Letters of acceptance (if no page proofs yet)
		• Page proofs (if In-Press)
		• Original copies of all publications
		• Copies of all presentations with conference program listing you as a presenter
		• Reviews of articles and books you authored
		• List of articles which cite your work

Table 2.2 Documentation to archive for tenure and promotion files

Domain	Experiences	Documentation (Paper and electronic as available and applicable)
Honors and Awards	• Honor societies • Scholarships and fellowships (merit based) • Research awards (from professional associations for publications, papers, or presentations) • Service awards (from professional associations or other organizations for outstanding service) • Teaching awards • Mentoring awards	• Copies of certificates and awards • Letter/notification of award • Award program • Press release, public announcement

Service	• Committee service: university, college, and department
	• Professional organizations
	  • Committee service
	  • Leadership
	  • Hosted academic event leadership or support (conferences, seminars, guest lectures)
	• Journal service
	  • Editorship (chief, associate, assistant, technical, production, etc.)
	  • Review board
	  • Ad hoc review (occasional, not a member of the standing board)
	• Community service
		• Committee appointment letters (if applicable)
		• Committee minutes
		• Hosted event programs
		• Leadership appointment letter (if applicable)
		• Copy of website, program, or letterhead which shows your title within an organization
		• Journal board appointment letter
		• Journal letter requesting review
		• Copy of website or journal which show you listed as reviewer

Table 2.2 Documentation to archive for tenure and promotion files, cont.

Table 2.2, while not exhaustive, will help guide you to know which of the many items that cross your desk each day are important to keep and file.

Reflect upon Conceptual and Thematic Organization

While physically organizing hard and electronic copies of relevant evaluative items and artifacts is critical to your success as an emerging scholar, it is also essential that you be able to organize your materials conceptually and thematically in order to support your teaching, research, and service narratives. Ultimately, you will use these items to illustrate key points in each of your narratives, and it is most likely that some of the items will be used multiple times in different sections of the same review, and possibly also in subsequent reviews. Many times unsuccessful promotion and tenure materials do not include this critical explanation. It seems that people find this step difficult, and some never complete it. Yet the solution is not difficult. Consider the following example, a dilemma which tenure and promotion applicants confront frequently: You need to use items to illustrate a particular aspect of your teaching philosophy in your annual review and mid-tenure portfolios not only as artifacts in a teaching award application, but also as part of your final tenure submission. So how does an emerging scholar begin to decide how to organize documentation of accomplishments and items illustrating key point for review narratives? Consider a concept map or graphic organizer to visualize how your work interrelates.

Since her pre-tenure days, Ann has always found it helpful to begin with a simple graphic organizer (or mind map) that she uses as a concept map to guide the writing of her narratives and as a placeholder to list documentation items and artifacts within her materials. This strategy concurs with the recommendations of many experts that graphics facilitate the writing process by organizing the writer's thoughts (Rico 1983). As an example of this strategy, let us consider how a simple outline may translate into a graphic organizer for a tenure application. Figure 2.2 illustrates how an assistant professor might organize her pre-tenure cover letter.

Kathy also developed simple graphics during the preparation of her promotion and tenure materials, but used them for different reasons. She created concept maps to illustrate different sections of her materials for the readers. Figures 2.3 and 2.4 display two graphics Kathy developed to illustrate her research efforts when she applied for tenure. She

1. INTRODUCTION AND THEME
2. RESEARCH AGENDA
   - Major focus areas
   - External and internal funding
   - Research application
   - Collaboration
   - Professional development
   - Next research goals
3. EDUCATIONAL PHILOSOPHY
   - Teaching
   - Assessment
   - Instruction development
   - Student evaluations
   - Professional development
   - Next teaching goals
4. SERVICE EFFORTS
   - Thematic connection
   - Impact: individual and institutional
   - Service goals and future
5. LOOKING FORWARD AND THANK YOU

Figure 2.2 Pre-tenure materials preparation:
Sample tenure cover letter outline and graphic organizer

developed Figure 2.3 because some faculty think pre-tenure faculty should focus on only one area of research. Her different areas of research consistently interrelate and inform one another. Therefore, to supplement her narrative explanation, she used a graphic (Figure 2.3) to illustrate how her three major strands of research merge.

Kathy also identified many of her individual research and grant projects within each domain in the graphic illustrated in Figure 2.4. She created one for each research domain, illustrating that they not only fit in the overall schema, but also had many connections. What is more, the reviewer will realize at a glance that there is both breadth and depth in the research conducted within these research areas. The fact that a mind map, concept map, or graphic organizer communicates this message swiftly provides valuable direction because readers face hundreds of pages of material to read during promotion and tenure review season. When we make our "case" for academic success more clear with accurate support and detail, our readers will be more likely to fully understand the significance and value of our record.

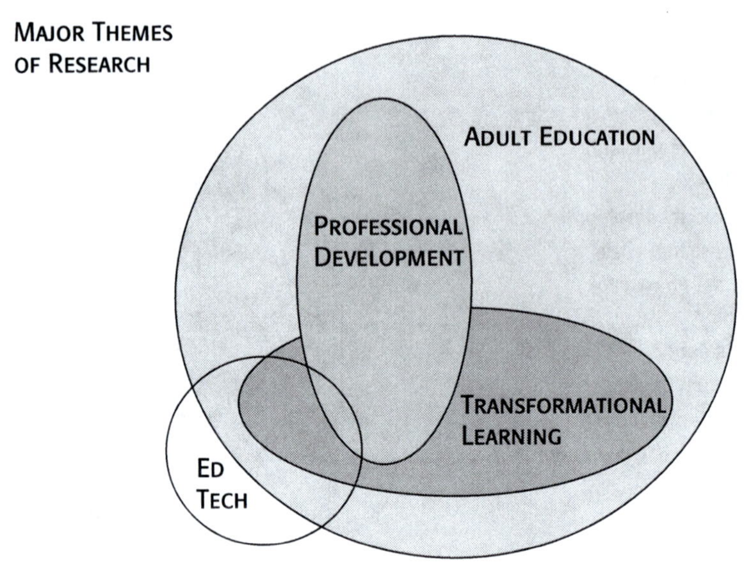

Figure 2.3 Pre-tenure materials: Concept map illustrating relationships among major themes of research

There are several reasons that this strategy of developing concept maps works. First, from the perspective of succeeding in our efforts, we must remember that the faculty and administrators who read our materials have different learning styles and preferences, just like our students (Donald 2003). Therefore, when we include a narrative and a graphic organizer to describe our accomplishments, we more effectively communicate with all readers. Second, the process of creating the graphic organizer (or concept map) helps us to understand better and further process our many different activities and accomplishments (Buzan 1999). By reflecting on our work in this manner, we likely develop new perspectives of the interrelationships among them, opportunities to connect our efforts for the readers, and ways to express our efforts' individual and collective impact (Moore 2012). All of these realizations will help us better communicate the value of our academic work to the audiences who will review us.

You may certainly create your concept map with pen and paper, but there are many simple electronic tools that can help produce professional figures. Some of these graphic organizer and concept map programs and websites include Prezi.com, Inspiration™, Freemind, Wise

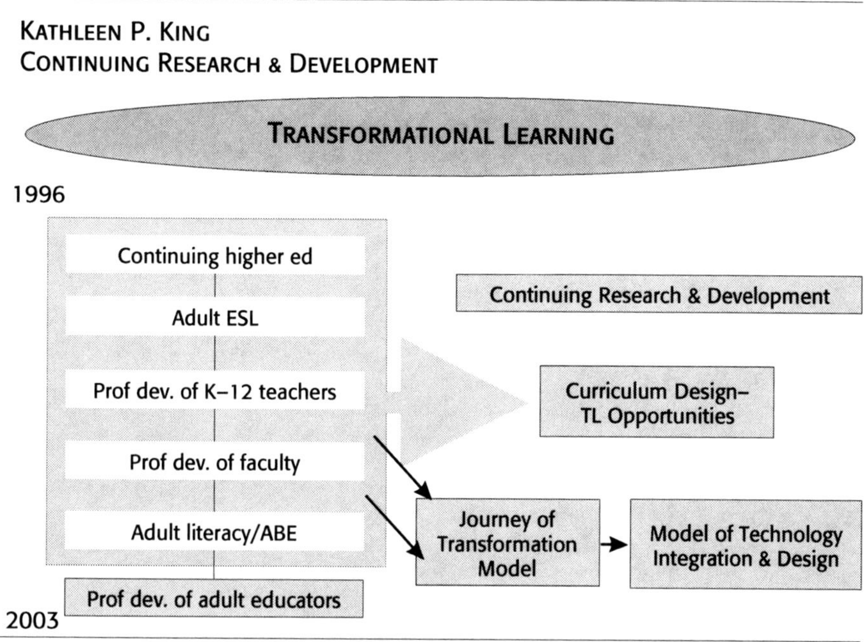

Figure 2.4 Pre-tenure materials: Detailed concept map of research

mapping.com, and Bubbl.us (https://bubbl.us). You can find many more just by searching the web for "free electronic graphic organizers."

Conclusion

This chapter provides some fundamental strategies for guiding emergent scholars' thinking and habits about navigating the "tenure track." The three critical landmarks identified, 1) Identify Sources of Information, 2) Plan the Experience and Plan to Gather, and 3) Reflect upon Conceptual and Thematic Organization, offer specific frames for effective action. The goal needs to be clear. One must not sacrifice tenure success for either the tyranny of the urgent or mountains of well-intentioned minutia.

In the remaining sections of the book, we continue to introduce detailed suggestions and tips regarding the major areas that emergent scholars must master. We believe you will find both new and familiar suggestions throughout the pages of this volume. The purpose remains to provide a consistent source of direction, support, and guidance as you continue on the journey you chose in the academy.

Category 1 Tips:

Taking Control of Your Career as a Scholar

1. Identify a formal or informal scholarship mentor at your institution to connect with at least every two months.

The first strategy we suggest is to identify a local scholarship mentor, primarily for guidance, accountability, and co-learning. They will not only provide specific and frequent direction about what activities are expected and valued, but can also be a sounding board for advice regarding decisions involved in some of the items in our 147 Tips. A valuable mentor will have successful experience in professional associations, research, teaching, and navigating your institution. As colleagues at different stages of their career and with varying skills, you can encourage each other in exchanging ideas, discovering opportunities, and advancing your careers. We always find that ideas sprout much more quickly when you have someone with whom to discuss them. Such mentoring relationships also provide opportunities for co-learning, which will bear mutual benefit and growth. If your institution does not have a formal mentoring program, or if you are not comfortable with your assigned mentor, don't hesitate to ask a senior colleague for advice and guidance. Most will be flattered by your request and more than willing to help. If you aren't sure who to ask, find out who in your institution has served on important review committees and start there.

2. Join relevant professional associations, receive journals, and attend conferences.

While it is important to become a member of well-chosen professional associations to build your career, we have always found that they can also be lifelines for emerging scholars for a wide variety reasons. We therefore encourage doctoral students to begin visiting and joining professional conferences early. As students, and often early career professors, you can join for reduced rates and receive journal publications, plus discounts on conferences and other publications. Professional associations are also sources of leads for positions, fellowships, research grants, and mentoring programs, to name just a few relevant opportunities. In addition, as you become involved in the associations you learn more about your field and may develop a community of colleagues.

3. Build your professional network with colleagues through your institution, conferences, associations, and more.

As alluded to above, professional colleagues are important for providing direction, guidance, feedback, and support as you develop your career. There is great benefit in building a network of colleagues across your institution and through conferences and associations, because they provide a diversity of perspectives, skills, and contacts. For instance, there are many situations where learning about examples of policies or procedures from across campus or across the country provides greater insight or clarity. Higher education is in a continuing state of change, a network of colleagues provides vital resources that may be helpful in coping with new situations. This network can also serve as an accountability community.

4. Build collaborative relationships with colleagues from your field and related fields.

Many times emerging and experienced scholars only consider collaborating with others within their field. However, maintaining such an exclusive approach may eliminate valuable opportunities from the future. Our appreciation of interdisciplinary studies increases as we see that the benefits are often profound. Consider that it is entirely similar to when you need to reach a different population for a research student —your colleagues in a different field might have access you do not. Similarly, different fields use different research methods, theories, models, and applications; by dialoguing with a diverse network of colleagues, you greatly increase the breadth of your options and resources.

5. Always spell check all your correspondence and submissions.

No matter what you are writing, whether it is email, memo, letter, or manuscript, it is essential to use spell and grammar check prior to distributing your written materials. Although typos and shorthand are often part of text messages and instant messaging, you can quickly damage your professional image with careless errors. Especially in written documents (electronic or paper), copies and forwards may find their way to a larger audience than intended. The safest and wisest strategy is to prepare your work to your best ability for a public audience and you will avoid both surprise and harm.

6. Develop or join a local research or writing collaborative.

Anyone who participates in local research or writing collaboratives can testify to the power of the experience for personal and professional development. A group of scholars with similar goals can create their own collaborative with the choice of at least two basic models: writing circle or collaborative. In the writing circle model, each individual contributes their current manuscript for the other members to evaluate and offer recommendations for improvement. Using the collaborative model, the group identifies a project which they are all interested in and have the skills to pursue. They divide the effort and work among them in order to accomplish the goal. In both models, we might tweak the old adage and observe: "Many minds make light work."

7. Successfully complete and keep your IRB certification updated (at your institution).

In order to conduct research within most accredited institutions, it is necessary to complete the Institutional Review Board application and process (which we will discuss later). However, the very first step in this process is completing the certification training and passing the tests. In addition, most institutions require everyone engaged in research to renew this certification every one or two years. Our recommendation is that students complete the training and tests as soon as possible and to keep their certification current throughout their careers. The great news is that most institutions make this process completely available online, allowing faculty to handle it at their own pace. This format provides great flexibility and maximum access. When will you begin yours?

8. Identify the characteristics you want in a paid professional scholarship coach (faculty or academic coach) to support your career development.

In some cases, faculty seeking tenure or promotion cannot find sufficient valuable mentoring support on their campus or among their network. At other times, the situation precludes being able to be open with a mentor who is from your same campus community. In these cases, identifying a paid professional scholarship coach, faculty, or academic coach can be a valuable choice. However, before entering into a relationship or contract for such services, we recommend that one clearly identify the characteristics and services you need provided. It is also wise to examine the credentials and experience of the individual to be certain they have both a theoretical understanding of what needs to be done and firsthand experience accomplishing the goals. An outside faculty coach can be an invaluable asset in the quest for position, tenure, or promotion when you need support beyond the time and expertise a volunteer can offer, or you need the confidentiality of a person outside your unit or institution.

9. Assess your cultural competence in communicating and respecting diverse colleagues and students (including but not limited to race, gender, class, LGBTQ, disability, international, language, etc.).

In our increasingly diverse global society, our professional standards and faculty expectations include cultural competence. As a faculty member, one needs to be able to teach and serve the educational needs of all students equitably. In addition, as both researcher and author, one needs to be mindful of not using stereotypes in examples and word choice. Most institutions have a diversity policy which guides campus activities. However, in order to understand fully what cultural competency means for the many different groups represented, one needs to reflect on prior assumptions and values. One needs to understand how to create truly safe learning environments for all students to express themselves without fear of harm. Many reference manuals (manuals of style such as APA, Chicago, MLA, etc) include guidelines regarding how to refer to different groups in writing and make language gender neutral in research and writing; these are good places to begin a review of the issue. It is also essential to keep seeking additional opportunities on campus and beyond to better understand the diverse groups you encounter or research.

Category 2 Tips:

Building a Research Agenda

10. Develop a research and publication agenda.

The first tip we share in this section is the overarching one of developing your research and publication agenda. All of the items in this category flow from this broad goal, as it includes examining and prioritizing several aspects of our preparation, skills, interests, and opportunities. In addition, one should review what other people in your institution pursue as their research agendas to determine if there is sufficient room for overlap.

Consider the situation in which there might only be three full-time faculty assigned to a comprehensive Chemistry department. If all of them pursued *only* Organic Chemistry related to blood gases, the department would lack the breadth of current research experience necessary to provide a well-rounded Chemistry education and research needs of the institution. On the other hand, if local industry had a large unmet demand in this area, and funded research and scholarships, these might be valid reasons to have such a faculty research interests. Understanding the context (the focus, mission, and tenured faculty of the institution, department, and program) provides important information about some choices scholars make regarding their research and publication agendas.

11. Identify and list the areas and strengths of your academic preparation and research interests.

Some of the strongest determinants in one's early research and publication agenda will be one's academic preparation focus and initial research interests. Indeed, for doctoral students, we recommend exploring research areas, building a foundation for your likely dissertation topic. In this manner, your work will build valuable background knowledge and perhaps data for your future effort. For early career faculty members, it is likely that your initial research and publication agenda will stem from your dissertation. Revisit the recommended future research sections of this document and your notes from your dissertation defense to see what leads you may uncover. We encourage faculty to explore more than one theme or focus of research in order to provide fresh perspectives, additional collaboration, publishing and funding opportunities.

12. Explore mining your current data further.

Sometimes we begin a research project with bold ambitions, but tire of the subject by the time we reach analysis and writing. After a brief period, perhaps two or three months, re-examine your data with a fresh perspective. You may discover that there is more valuable information hidden there. Specifically, if you had used one method of analyzing your data, choosing a different method, test, or set of tests may yield further findings.

13. Examine natural extensions of your past and current work.

If you had explored your research with one sample, what about others? Could you examine the same, or similar, research questions with different research methods? Could you develop a Phase II or III of your study by accessing or obtaining more data in different ways? Mixed-methods research in particular is a valuable framework for this approach. Sequential mixed methods research would be the particular category of research applicable in these cases. Once the initial study is completed, the researcher then gathers additional data with a different research method. If you are not familiar with mixed-methods research, turn to this volume's resource appendix for recommended sources.

14. Rate items based on your interest level, the difficulty of conducting research (approval, funding, etc.), and availability of data.

Just as one might make a list of pros and cons in decision making, why not create a table that facilitates ranking your research options according to your level of interest, and the difficulty of gaining funding, approval, or data? Frequently, when we use more objective measures to itemize choices, we discover that a preferred choice becomes more apparent. Alternatively, one may pair research efforts so that they balance one another. In order to maintain a steady flow of grants and publications, you might select projects which are easier to access, fund, etc. But having a few of those in process will afford the opportunity to pursue that exciting project that takes more time or has little funding accompanying it. We do not have to exclude any of our research ideas; we just wisely balance them for the greater goal of building our scholarly agenda and our record.

15. Explore current publications and grant opportunities to determine your most viable areas.

As you advance in your decision making process, consider the availability of both funding and publications. Are certain topics more widely funded at this time, while other topics are less frequently the topic of Request for Proposals (official notice of availability of a grant)? Some major publications in your field may illuminate these trends by listing calls for papers for conferences, special issues of journals, and funding. Which of these topics are you best qualified to pursue within the allocated timeframe? Are they annual postings, so that you may prepare for next year? If so, record them in your calendar now and backtrack from the due date to see when you need to begin preparations. Perhaps there are opportunities to partner with like-minded colleagues from your writing circle, mentor a younger colleague, or network to strengthen a viable submission and broaden its appeal. Think strategically about your research agenda.

16. Complete a table (see Appendix) that lists all your research projects and identifies what stages you are at and expected completion dates for each stage.

Use the table found in Appendix B to record all your research projects. In this chart, you must track the stages of development as you progress, as well as your target dates for completion. While the completion date might be determined by a deadline, your intermediary dates may be based on your situation and choices. This table illustrates your freedom to organize your time and efforts to achieve your goals. In addition, remember the old saying: "If you do not have a target, you are sure to always miss it."

While you might not ever share this actual document with a committee, it is invaluable to help plan your work and keep you on target.

There are countless times when you will find you refer to this tracking table. Here are a few examples: when updating your CV, completing annual reports, tenure or promotion applications, writing personal narratives about your career (which many grant applications require), sharing what research you have in progress, or determining if it is time to contact a journal editor about your review.

17. Identify two to four conferences where you can present/publish different results of your research.

Based on the review of call for papers and your literature research, identify two to four research conferences where you may present your work for the next few years. You should select at least one top tier conference, but also be sure to include a regional or state conference as well if you are a doctoral student. Examining the leadership list of the organization should provide some direction about the value and rank of the conference. Mark these dates in your calendar as tentative until accepted. Examine prior proposals or presentation materials to determine the audience, style, and format needed, and address these in your proposal and final work.

18. Identify two to three journals where you can publish different results from your research.

Much as in the manner described above, now is the time to identify two to three refereed journals (and their websites) based on calls for papers. We always suggest that students and early career faculty review sample issues and articles from the last three years for several reasons. One can learn about the tone of the conversation, the interest of the audience, and the nature of the recent scholastic conversation, and ensure that your submission will fit well.

19. Recognize that your research and publication agenda can be flexible.

As much as we like to use tables and charts to plan our work and deadlines, we understand that life gets in the way sometimes. Therefore, flexibility in our timelines is a powerful characteristic when we identify our own intermediary or final deadlines. While we can elect to move the deadlines for ourselves or collaborators, examining the tables first will demonstrate an immediate ripple effect. The planning table reveals the interlocking nature of work more explicitly, thus guiding us to stay on track or regain our planned pace.

20. Consider new trends in your discipline or field that you can explore.

Contrary to popular belief, professors are not all-knowing. The most productive faculty are those who are life-long learners and who thrive on new opportunities to develop their knowledge base and skills. What new trends could inform your current work? Are there new trends about which you have questions? Currently, knowledge and research grow faster than ever before; as academic researchers, we cannot afford to tune out new developments and rely solely on our doctoral preparation. New developments may serve as vital parts of your growing research agenda.

Category 3 Tips:

General Writing Tips

21. Explain the structure of your work to your readers.

Advanced organizers are a literary tool to disclose to readers what will happen in the next pages or chapter. Especially in long academic documents such as journal articles and book chapters, they are indispensable in helping your work flow and maintaining the reader's focus. You can find examples of advanced organizers in this book. Look for times in which we introduce a specific number of characteristics and points. Notice that we often list them first and then in the following sentences explain them more in depth.

22. Write with the flow; do not stop for minor details in your manuscript when you are progressing well.

We all know how difficult it is to establish a good flow of thought and writing in our academic work, right? Well, once you have it in motion, for goodness sake, do not interrupt it! We find that by allowing the flow of thought and production to continue unimpeded, we make much more progress than if we try to correct every word and look up every citation in the midst of writing. Establish conventions to identify that you need to return to a section to correct grammar or spelling or insert citations, examples, etc. You will be surprised at how your production increases and how you feel better about the progress of your work!

23. Use the "cite here" strategy while writing. Incorporate citations and references, or markers for them, as you write for clarity and completeness.

One of Kathy's small strategies that other people rave about is the "cite here" method. This trick is one of the ways she maintains the flow of her writing. When the writing flows, Kathy does not stop to search out citations and references: instead she inserts yellow highlighted text with the name of the author, and perhaps the year. Alternatively, if she cannot quite recall the reference, she only inserts "cite here" in yellow highlight. This practice allows her thought flow to continue quickly and uninterrupted, while capturing her intention to add additional material later. This practice thrills students and faculty because we can all identify with our thoughts being derailed while hunting down a reference for our work. Instead of us constantly starting and stopping all the time, this trick allows greater academic writing efficiency.

24. Determine priority and timeline for your writing project in your current schedule.

As an emerging scholar, you know that writing has a very high priority for your career advancement, but are you really acting like it does? By simply listing the things you have to do today and this week, and then prioritizing them, you can then make a better decision and commitment to the time you need to accomplish your wiring. When the tyranny of the urgent again raises innumerable interruptions, return to your list and determine where you can schedule to address the item/concern. In fact, it is easy to postpone many of the issues for which we interrupt our writing activity for a few hours or the next day. Focus is a major difficulty for all writers (Moore 2012); therefore, having strategies to cope with the many potential interruptions of our professional lives is very effective. This tip is an essential aspect of "working your plan," which we mentioned in Chapter 1.

25. Determine your need for and compatibility with potential co-authors and co-editors carefully.

While it may seem like fun or politically beneficial to collaborate with someone on a written project, evaluate your choices carefully. You want to talk through where the writing project stands in both of your professional and personal commitments, how much time and when (timeline) you are willing to dedicate to it, and your philosophy of collaboration. Does your colleague consider that you both will view and edit every word composed for the project? Or would they prefer to write individual sections and later edit them together into a single document? Two other essential elements include building the expectation and mechanisms for constructive feedback and accountability. You need to come to an agreement about how the project and process will proceed prior to beginning, or else it may be disrupted, prolonged, or abandoned.

26. If collaborating on a writing project, develop a simple but clear list of responsibilities and deadlines.

Given the breadth of issues listed above, it is reasonable to develop a list of responsibilities and timeline for your project. Agreeing to this at the beginning provides accountability. A written document can make the commitment and responsibility much more concrete and help achieve more realistic decision making. For example, time frames should only change by mutual agreement. Certainly colleagues need to appreciate that unexpected events and demands happen in everyone's life; therefore respecting one another's needs is essential in coping with disruptions. However, there has to be enough commitment to the project for you both to accomplish it.

27. Explore writing books to cultivate different writing styles, literary formats, chapter openings, storytelling, etc.

For those of us academics who are not language experts, it is beneficial to continue to build our writing skills in several ways. One fun and instructive approach is to identify books and articles about academic writing. In this effort, one should not focus only on how to write academic articles and research papers, but instead the mechanisms and a style of writing. We find that as we write more, our practice develops. If we are not receiving feedback, direction on the best ways to improve, or new styles to try, from where will the valuable input come? In the appendix of this volume, you will find a list of resources for many of your needs as an emerging scholar. One of those resources includes a list of books we have found helpful in improving our writing.

28. Identify excellent fiction and nonfiction authors to read at leisure while engaged in writing in order to build your repertoire of diverse writing structures, styles, vehicles, and vocabulary.

A tip related to the previous one, is to include excellent literature in your personal and professional reading. Much like our parents used to remind us "You are what you eat," so it is true that "you write what you read." As we read the classics and other excellent authors, we discover new literary vehicles, improve our vocabulary and content knowledge, and absorb new grammatical constructions. In addition, your personal reading can serve as a release or recreational outlet for you in the writing process. Our minds continue to process our writing needs when we engage in other activities. Turning our attention to other subjects temporarily can refresh and, at times, enlighten us.

29. If you have known difficulties in your writing, have a "punch list" of items you check before the final stage of development.

None of us is perfect in the writing process and we all have our idiosyncratic difficulties in writing. We find keeping a list of those errors others continue to identify as you review your work, can expedite the editing process. In factories, they used to create a punch list of all the items that needed to be accomplished or double-checked before a project was completed. Applying this method to our writing, we make a list of our difficulties and use it as a checklist during editing. Rather than trying to remember to review all those miscellaneous items of grammar, style, spelling and punctuation, etc., it is much more efficient to have a standing list that ensures consistent action. Which are your grammatical weaknesses: verb agreement, homonyms, comma splices, or run-on sentences?

If you are not aware of your grammatical habits of error, the next time you have work proofread, make a list of the most frequent errors identified. This personalized list builds greater efficiency and better writing habits. For example, Kathy finds it easier to review the entire manuscript only looking for checklist errors #1 and #2. She corrects all those items and then proceeds to the next one or two items on the checklist. This strategy helps focus our proofreading and usually results in more accurate writing and quicker corrections. Over time, most people using this practice internalize the correct grammar practice and can add new items to their checklist to advance their writing skills further. Make and use your personal punch list to begin conquering those annoying foibles consistently.

30. Have at least two colleagues read your final manuscript for content, logic, grammar, and proofreading.

Who are the colleagues that you trust to be both discreet and accomplished? Identify two such scholars, local or distant, to serve as your usual academic reviewers. It is important that you explain what you would like them to comment on in your work and to determine how many per month or year they have time to review. See if they are comfortable with "track changes" features of word processing, as this will be efficient for them and convenient for you to review changes and incorporate them into your final work. These colleagues will be invaluable in providing honest and constructive feedback about your work prior to submission. Consider how much time you will save submitting a reviewed paper or manuscript to a publisher. You may eliminate an entire round of rewrites. Also, consider how you can provide a compensatory service for your reviewer colleagues. Determine which skills you have that might benefit them—perhaps in technology, statistical analysis, or literary research. They are investing time in your career; be a generous colleague and support them as well.

31. Create a master list of recommendations from your colleagues, identify how you will correct those items, and edit the paper prior to submission.

Many scholars have no idea how to streamline incorporating all the changes and recommendations they received from colleagues or peer reviewers. The solution really is quite straightforward. Make a bullet list to summarize each point identified in the reviews. Examine the list, analyze and synthesize it—what is the overall directive? What are the trends of issues identified? List the specific items for each trend which need addressing. You now have your punch list of edits. This list will be your checklist for revising your work.

Bonus tip: If items show up on these review lists several times across projects, add that item to your master punch list (prior tip), which should be reviewed *prior to* initial peer reviews!

32. Separate your feelings from the critique and editing process as much as possible.

We know it is difficult at first, but it is essential that emerging scholars learn to remove their personal feelings from the reviews of their academic work. The critiques are evaluations of your current written product. They are not evaluations of your character or worth! One simple fact that helps many early scholars is that most accomplished authors say they can wallpaper their office with all the rejection letters they receive. Writing for publication is a process, and that process is distinct for every publication. Be encouraged that people take the time to review and critique your work. Garner the valuable information from those reviews and implement them in your current and future work. If there are any nasty comments, and unfortunately sometimes there are, ignore them and vow that you will not do the same to emerging scholars when you are the reviewer.

Category 4 Tips:

Developing and Writing Your Literature Review

33. Consider the major theoretical works which underpin your research topic. These are foundational topics for your literature review.

Many emerging scholars struggle with writing good literature reviews. Part of the issue may be in differing expectations from prior professors. Nonetheless, there is a standard of excellent work in academia to which you should aspire. The place to begin is to determine which theoretical works would provide a comprehensive foundation for the discussion of your topic. There will often be three or four theoretical areas, which the author needs to investigate and represent fully.

Kathy grew up in the Northeastern United States and she knows the importance of a solid foundation. During the winter, the ground freezes before thawing in the spring. If you do not anchor your house's foundation well enough, it will shift or at least crack substantially and damage the house, likely to ruins. She tells her students and colleagues to think of the literature review as so many concrete blocks to join through their analysis and create a substantial foundation for their research to stand. Given this analogy, which blocks would be the best to use for your paper or project's theoretical foundation? Which areas will provide the strongest basis for the research questions you will pursue?

34. Articulate the themes you identify and synthesize in your literature review.

While reading the scores of publications related to your theoretical foundation, several phenomena will occur. First, you will realize that the same authors' works arise continually. Second, you will not read anything new about the topic. Third, you will discover specific sources emerging as the "bedrock" of your topic. That is, these sources are the first occurrences of the same concept or specific citations. At this point, you are ready to "scan the landscape of the literature" and evaluate which themes you recognize. You want to be aware of groups of content and perspectives *within* each body of literature, in addition to differences between them. Such analysis and synthesis are the cornerstones of excellent literature reviews.

35. Do not present your work solely in chronological order; identify themes instead.

Many times, we will see people submit literature reviews that are not fully developed. Instead of a synthesis of theory and research across the varied foundational topics, usually they submit a chronological discussion of the field's research. When we examine such work, we recognize that their best categorization is either as annotated bibliographies or the history of the topic.

You can avoid this problem entirely by following the previous tip. Using that strategy you develop a comparison and contrast across and within the areas. Moreover, you organize the literature by the themes the paper's author identified. When you write your literature review with this structure of themes, rather than chronology, it is truly a unique and worthwhile contribution. Such analysis and synthesis of the paper's theoretical constructs provides a robust foundation for research.

36. Do not create a patchwork paper. Avoid overusing direct quotes.

Have you ever read a paper or literature review in which you never gain the sense that you "hear" the voice of the author? Usually this situation occurs when they overuse direct quotations. Remember when you write your literature review that the point is to process the existing literature based on *your* fresh understanding. Therefore, your readers (and the reviewers) want to read your perspective on the literature and the connections you seek to make. They do not want to read an endless series of direct quotes by other people strung together. Professional manuals and writing books have a name for this construction: "a patchwork paper." In fact, if you think about it, it is a much weaker level of analysis and writing than a true literature review. As mentioned, the author has presented only raw data/literature, instead of sharing an analysis and interpretation.

A related issue to this situation is that writers may feel inadequate to share their interpretations, or not be empowered to do so. At this point in your professional development, you need to begin to discover how to express your voice in your writing. The strategies shared in this and the previous tip are designed to guide authors in building their unique understanding and supported positions, and thus their voice and confidence.

37. Develop a concept map to illustrate the relationship of factors or themes in our literature review.

A useful strategy to assist in the analysis and synthesis of a literature review is for the author to develop a concept map or graphic organizer to illustrate the relationship among the examined themes (Buzan 1989; Rico 1983). The concept map may be a simple figure that illustrates how the themes overlap, build on one other, and differentiate, for instance. Common formats include Venn diagrams, flow charts, hierarchical charts, and hub and spoke configurations; however, there are myriad possibilities. Creating a concept map in this process serves at least two valuable roles. First, it helps the author identify the relationship among the themes using visual constructs, rather than texts. Second, it serves as a valuable device to compliment the textual description of the relationship to the reader.

38. Explain the concept map in your literature review.

Based on the benefits of a concept map, it is helpful to include it in your manuscript. However, if you do so, you must explain it adequately. We think of the explanation, or narrative, about the figure as walking the reader through the concept map. Regarding communication and learning methods, what happens when we use a concept map as a figure in our manuscripts is that we appeal to multiple intelligences and various parts of readers' brains.

39. Consider gaps in the literature which can be addressed.

One of the classic ways to leverage a thorough literature review is to identify a gap, or gaps, in the literature and to use that as the focus of your discussion. For instance, if you examine three areas within one theoretical area and none of them address a specific dimension of issues, you have discovered a valuable omission. The next step would be to use the existing literature and research to construct hypotheses to address that area and potentially design a solution. Of course, it is essential that your literature review be complete and thorough before making statements about the absence of anything. You may discuss your findings with a colleague or ask the librarians to run searches for the information prior to committing your reputation to this position. If you find through triangulating your process that gaps exist, you can proceed with much greater confidence.

40. Consider a conceptual model, which can be developed to explain the literature review.

Sometimes, literature review work will result in the development of a conceptual model. A model may be a natural way to explain the relationship and dynamic of the literature review findings. For instance, if we examine all the theoretical issues related to a specific topic, we might observe not only themes or categories, but also specific ways in which these elements relate. You may begin by sketching your draft model on paper and then use one of many program options to develop a more professional design. Suggested programs include iDraw™, Inspiration™, PowerPoint™, iPhoto™, Adobe Illustrator™ or Photoshop™, or even the drawing features within your word processor.

41. Make sure you list every work you cite in your manuscript in the reference list.

It is important that you list every article, manuscript, journal article, document, etc. that you cite in your manuscript in the reference list. Once emerging scholars begin exploring the literature more fully, and relying on the citations and references provided by other authors, they usually begin to realize their critical role. In exactly the same manner, your readers will depend on you to provide complete and accurate reference details for the literature to which you refer.

As an author, how does one check for accuracy in this situation? We use a two stage process we call "reconciling the references" when we proofread our manuscripts. The first stage includes this tip; the second stage is the next tip. To complete stage one, we print a list of the references and then read through the manuscript and check off whether every citation is included in that list. We note missing ones by writing the author and year on the list and add them into the manuscript before proceeding to step two (the next tip).

42. Make sure you cite every work you mention in the reference list of your manuscript in the paper.

The corollary to the previous tip is verifying that you do not have entries in your reference list that are not cited in the manuscript. Most publications require this type of listing, which is literally a reference list. If they ask for a bibliography, it would then include all the sources you consulted.

In order to efficiently conduct step two of our reference reconciliation (see the tip above), we print out a fresh copy of the current references. Next, with the document open in our word processor, we move the cursor to the beginning and engage the search function to determine if the first reference entry is included in the body of the manuscript. If it is, we check it off. If it is not, we cross it off the list of references. In the process, we also double-check the consistent spelling of authors' names and the dates of each publication. When we finish searching for all the reference entries, we then return to the list in the word processor and delete the extras, and fix any other errors we identified.

43. Review the criteria for a literature review in your discipline and evaluate yours with these guidelines as a rubric.

Many disciplines have unique expectations or criteria for a literature review. Therefore, in order for your manuscript to be well accepted, it needs to follow those guidelines. First, identify whether your discipline, academic program, or department have guidelines or recommendations for outstanding literature reviews. If such guidelines exist, obtain a copy to use as a guideline for your work. Finally, when you prepare to proofread your literature review, use the guidelines as a rubric and evaluate your work alongside it. This strategy provides specific direction to improve your work prior to external review.

Category 5 Tips:

Presenting at Conferences

44. Identify the professional and academic conferences which fit your content area(s) and method(s) of research.

When we work on our research, we always have in mind not only venues for publication, but also conference presentations. Indeed, it is helpful to present your work at conferences prior to submitting for publication, because you can gain valuable feedback and insight about your analysis, discussion, and interpretation. With these purposes as the premise, select the conferences where you believe you may gain the most relevant and best feedback for your work. How do you determine which conferences suit your specific needs? First, we consider whether a professional association or conference publishes or sponsors the journal within which we aspire to publish. If not, we determine which conferences our target journal's audience attends in order that we might engage with them. Third, if we also do not know where they attend, we identify the best conferences in the discipline that welcome scholars at our level of expertise.

45. If pursuing tenure or promotion, print evidence of the selected conferences' use of the peer review process.

Whether you are a doctoral student or in the tenure and promotion process, be certain to print evidence that the conference to which you submit uses peer review. It is much easier to find this information at this time, than it will be two, three, or ten years from now when you urgently need it. Why is this evidence important? Without evidence of the peer review process, your hard work may not be acknowledged by your review committee. Where do you find this information? Common places to discover these details include the call for proposals, the authors'/presenters' guidelines, the conference description, and the conference website.

46. Identify evidence of the national/international reputation and standing of the conference.

In the same vein as the previous tip, we also need to collect written documentation regarding the national/international scope and reputation of conferences. While academics in your field may be familiar with the level of scholarship accepted by a specific conference, other professionals who serve on tenure, promotion, or search committees may not be. Therefore, use those same sources listed above to document the reputation, scholarship, and standing of this professional venue. In addition to making a copy or printing the information, we also recommend scanning it into your electronic portfolio.

47. Identify the guidelines for authors and determine which type of submission fits your needs and time frame.

The call for papers is usually quite lengthy for professional and academic conferences because they include details regarding many types and formats of submissions. Some conferences only request proposals for lecture style presentations, others include panels, roundtable discussions, poster sessions, workshops, discovery sessions, "lightening rounds," and more. In order to make the best choice, gain the most from the opportunity, and improve your chances of acceptance, academics need to understand the definitions and criteria used by this specific conference for each format available. If you do not fully understand a specific format you must use to submit your manuscript, contact the designated people and ask them to answer your questions. In addition, you may also consult colleagues in your institution or network that might have submitted and/or attended this conference. Do yourself a favor and understand the submission categories; you do not want a rejection letter because of lack of understanding.

48. Learn how to fulfill all requirements of the proposal submission guidelines.

Some conference proposal submission guidelines contain many specific requirements. Whether it is specific criteria, word count, page count, conference theme, font size, submission delivery system, or other items, be certain you understand and comply with/fulfill them all. Usually, there are good reasons for each one of those requirements. In addition, when people submit proposals without following the guidelines, it suggests several traits to the reviewers. Do you want to be seen as being careless, lacking attention to detail, refusing to comply with guidelines, or not understanding your field/discipline? Of course, none of these attributes reflects favorably for academics. Following the guidelines is a small but highly visible way to demonstrate your professional commitment.

49. Read the program descriptions and several papers or presentations from previous years of the conference in order to learn about the audience.

In our experience, few people take this extra step to ensure greater success for their conference proposals. With so much information now posted on publicly accessible websites, and more scholarly papers being freely and instantaneously available through our institutional library databases, it is often easy to read the program descriptions and/or papers prior to writing your own. Not only will this activity of reviewing an exemplar help you understand what the conference reviewers expect, but it also illustrates the nature and tenor of the accepted proposals and the interests of the audience.

50. Address the conference theme clearly in your proposal submission.

Conference committees usually spend substantial time and energy to create a theme for their conference. They select themes in order to develop a common general focus for the conference event. Therefore, when submitting a proposal, be certain to address the theme in significant ways. For instance, you may open with statements as to how your proposal is valuable for the conference and its participants. In order to accomplish this goal, you also need to investigate the literature for meaningful ways your topic relates to the conference theme.

51. Consider attending the conference prior to submitting a proposal, in order to better understand the context and expectations.

One of the best ways to learn the culture and focus of a conference is to attend it before submitting a proposal. When using this strategy, it helps to develop concrete goals and plan specific activities during the conference. Attending different formats of sessions is a good strategy, as you learn the benefits and limitations of each. In addition, this approach reveals the culture, expectations, and specific protocols used. Attend sessions, watch, listen, talk to new and old colleagues, and reach beyond your comfort zone to discover new opportunities. All of this information will enable you to make proposal submission choices in future years.

52. Be certain to bring business cards with your contact information on them to the conference with you.

We encourage professionals at all levels of their career to design and print business cards as soon as possible. The business card is the academic's currency for networking and collaboration. Currently business cards are very inexpensive if ordered online. This may require urgency and awareness, however, because ordering the business cards online requires advanced planning as the development and delivery process stretches across several weeks. If you do not have time or money for this solution, there are at least two options available. Print business cards in black and white or color on stock card paper, or, as a last resort, copy paper. Whichever backup format you use, we suggest a pastel color of paper or card stock in order to stand out. When you distribute these temporary cards, just mention to people that your formal cards are not yet ready or that you ran out of your official cards. The final option is to collect other people's email addresses and initiate contact as soon as possible after you meet them.

53. Review the conference program prior to attending to develop a strategy and look for tips for first time attendees.

Attending a new conference can be confusing and even overwhelming; therefore, advanced planning is important. Smaller conferences may email a conference program to registered participants and presenters, whereas larger conferences often have a searchable database and planning feature. Whichever situation you encounter, search for an orientation or first time attendees' session. These sessions can be very helpful in explaining the different types of sessions, networking, and professional development opportunities available during the events. Another strategy is to think about what type of sessions will assist your professional development. Sessions about your research topics, research methods, and/or courses you teach are all immediate options. Conferences are also wonderful opportunities to expand your knowledge base in each of these areas and others.

54. Develop a strategy as to how you will select sessions at the conference—by theme, strand, etc.

As you select sessions, you might use themes, strands, or whatever demarcation the conference uses to identify related sessions. Not only will this allow you to focus your attention, but also you may develop professional contacts and relationships with others who attend the sessions. Building a network of colleagues who research and specialize in the same field as your work can be invaluable for many reasons. Following a series of similar sessions at a conference also provides a more extensive professional development experience than a single session. As you can see, you have many options for how you chose to benefit as you attend professional conferences.

55. Plan your proposal so that the presentation will provide feedback on your research or model.

When you have the opportunity to present at a conference, this opportunity can greatly advance your research and publication agenda if planned appropriately. Many conferences allow presenters to decide on the specifics of their presentation. If your session is a roundtable or poster session, it already is a wonderful platform for you to briefly present your key findings verbally and in print while dialoguing with participants about their perspective and questions related to your work. However, we find that session participants enjoy activities, even in lecture style presentations. Therefore, we try to design a culturally appropriate activity that helps participants to consider the issues, dilemmas, struggles, or problems embedded in the presentation topic. The participants experience the topic in an interactive manner and contribute their perspective as the presentation unfolds. You, as the presenter, face new questions and perspectives from your colleagues. This strategy exhibits the benefits of academic dialogue.

56. If the conference does not publish full proceedings for your 20–30 page presentation or paper, transform it into a journal manuscript submission.

Some conferences do not publish full research papers, but you can plan to use the opportunity to advance your final publication while also having a conference presentation for your CV. Before you submit to a conference, you should see if they publish a full proceeding or select papers for journal publication so that you can plan accordingly. If they do not, then as you plan your presentation and paper, also complete the steps to identify a journal for publication and prepare a parallel manuscript for that audience and related criteria. The feedback you gain through your conference presentation (tips above) will guide the final development of your journal submission.

Category 6 Tips:

Publishing in Refereed Journals

57. Maintain a regular writing schedule for journal articles.

As a new assistant professor, Kathy asked a senior colleague how to succeed with writing. He said, "Write every day." This advice is golden and yet terribly difficult. When you are flooded with teaching classes, conference and grant proposal deadlines, and book chapter invitations, it will be tempting to let your research writing slide. The reality is that the stakes for a single activity could not be higher than this one: if you do not write the articles, journals will not publish them, and you will obtain neither tenure nor academic promotion. All your teaching, advising, collaboration, committee meetings, and class preparation will be in vain, because you did not stay constant with your journal article writing commitment. Leaving fear and panic behind us, let us consider the successful route your will choose.

Other helpful tips on this topic mentioned in this book include strategies for tracking your research, writing, and submissions, making appointments in your calendar for writing, joining or starting a writing circle, and more. However, they all begin with a commitment by you and your family: you to designate and revere that time, and your family to value you the time and space. Whether you find it best to schedule your writing time early, mid, or late in the day, build a routine, and eventually a habit, of writing *for your journal articles* each day. The writing process includes not only writing, but also endless editing. Therefore, we all need to invest many hours in writing to create each successful publication. When we continue to write daily, we produce an extraordinary volume of publishable material compared to writing in sporadic efforts or periodic binges. Steady wins the race; and as an added boon, your writing will flow more fluidly as you make it a daily practice. Enjoy the creativity of writing and explore some of the writing resources listed in the Appendix for additional encouragement and ideas.

58. Investigate the references you cite in your manuscript for likely journal submission venues.

These sources may provide you new leads for journals or edited book series that will be likely places to publish your research. If they are publishing other articles/chapters/papers on topics related to yours, then they may well understand the value of your work and manuscript.

59. Do not hastily contact the journal editor before submitting or while waiting to hear about a decision.

It is common for publishing decisions to take longer than anticipated. You should wait patiently to hear about your article. For your best interests, please refrain from contacting the editor once you submit the article until about two months *after they indicated you would hear from them*. (Note: This means six months after your submission, if they indicated you would receive feedback in four months.)

If you have heard nothing by this point, you may send a very brief and polite email pointing out the timeframe and requesting information about the review progress and estimated time for a decision. Repeat this timeline at the same interval (two months beyond the expected date) with caution and finesse. Remember, you hope to publish in these journals many times; therefore, you want to build a positive relationship with the editor.

60. Always submit a cover letter with your journal manuscript.

When submitting your manuscript, you should always include a cover letter specifying the call for papers/articles to which you are responding, the title of your article, and your contact information. This cover letter, whether a hard copy or electronic, serves as a tracking document for both you and the journal staff.

Your cover letter should be courteous, brief, and upbeat. Never press editors for a rapid decision in your initial cover letter. Instead, quite the opposite approach is appropriate: consider briefly expressing appreciation for their service, time, and contribution to the field. (Most journal editors do not receive any compensation for the extensive work they provide authors.)

61. Identify the journals that fit your content and methods of research.

The first step in getting your articles published in refereed journals is to identify journals that fit your content and methods of research. You will also need to determine who the primary audience is for each of your articles and select target journals accordingly. Journals' websites as well as hard copies of the journals have information about each of these areas. Before searching blindly for potential journals, it is a good idea for emerging scholars to seek suggestions from colleagues who have more experience with publishing in refereed articles.

62. If pursuing tenure or promotion, verify and print evidence that the journal is peer reviewed and add it to your tenure materials.

Don't rely on word-of-mouth to document that the journals you select for publication are refereed. You will want to print and keep documentation regarding the article review process for each of the journals you target for your articles. This should be done simultaneously with submission. You will need documentation for tenure and promotion and don't want to take the chance that the information will not be available when you need it.

63. Identify the impact factor of the journal to determine the standard of scholarship.

Depending on the standards of scholarship of your institution, or those of the institutions you aspire to be employed by, you will need to pay attention to the impact factor of your targeted journals. A journal's impact factor is based on the number of times its articles are cited within a specified time frame. Other factors that you should consider that are related to journal quality include the journal's acceptance/rejection rate, reputation among scholars in the field, and overall circulation.

64. Never send a "query letter" to academic journal editors.

It is usually not necessary to send a query letter prior to submitting your article to a targeted journal. If you have done your homework in advance, you should have a good idea of whether your article is appropriate for submission. Instances where a query letter would be appropriate include proposals to submit articles for a themed issue of a journal or requests for more detailed information regarding a particular area of focus.

65. Review the guidelines for authors and determine if the journal is appropriate for your manuscript submission.

It is important to become familiar with your target journal's specific focus before submitting your article. Otherwise you may waste time better invested focusing on a more appropriate journal. In addition to reviewing copies of the journal itself to understand the nature and tenor of the manuscripts accepted, you should also consult the author's guidelines for information regarding the types of articles published. This includes the range of topics considered, as well as the nature of the articles, such as whether they should be based on the results of original research or if theoretical or literature based submissions are acceptable.

66. Read prior issues of the journal to which you intend to submit.

As you review these recent issues of the journal, notice the topics of focus of the articles, types of research methods, length, formality, and format. These characteristics are important in guiding you—not only in selecting the most appropriate venue for your manuscript, but also in preparing it in the style and format consistent with the publication's needs. Both benefits will increase the likelihood of good research's acceptance the first time submitted.

67. Learn how to fulfill all requirements of the authors' guidelines.

Follow journal instructions regarding which stylistic guidelines to follow. You can access style manuals either by hard copy or through the internet. In addition, your institution's library website will most likely have online tutorials, help sheets, and workshops available to assist you with stylistic concerns. You will also need to adhere to author guidelines regarding minimum and maximum page limits and inclusion of tables and figures.

68. If you are sincerely uncertain whether your article will fit a given journal (not fishing for pre-approval), submit an abstract to the editor and ask for an opinion.

It really helps to obtain this guidance early on, since you want to write the manuscript for your specific journal audience in as much as possible. Often if editors indicate that your manuscript abstract indicates the article would not be viable for their journal, they may offer, or if asked will provide, one or more suggestions of other publications or conferences. If you do take this approach, be sure to have an accurate estimate of when the manuscript will be ready for submission, because the editor(s) may have immediate opportunities for consideration. Please remember most editors serve without compensation, and thank them for their expertise, time, and generosity with you. In all these interactions, you are building professional relationships that eventually interconnect.

69. Organize your manuscript around the major headings for a research article.

With some variation, research articles for publication in refereed journal articles are typically organized around the following major headings: Title Page, Abstract, Background or Introduction, Method, Results, Discussion, and References. Each section should be comprehensive enough to stand on its own so that a reader interested in a particular aspect could choose to look at only that section.

70. Develop and refine the text for each section of the article.

Develop an informative title for your article and create a title page that includes the title, your name, and your institutional affiliation. Format for the title page differs according to the particular style (APA, MLA, etc.) you are following. Your abstract should be written last, despite its placement right after the title page. Most journals recommend that abstracts be no longer than about 200–250 words. Your abstract should provide a brief introduction to your topic, an overview of the method used (including participants), and a concise summary of your results. You should also include key words with your abstract. The Background or Introduction section of your paper is where you introduce the reader to your topic, provide a rationale for the study, outline the theoretical or conceptual framework guiding the study, and present your research questions. Be sure to establish a connection to what is known in the field by citing relevant literature in your Introduction. In the Method section, you should clearly lay out the design of your study and the procedures you followed to conduct it. This should include a description of your participants, as well as any instruments you may have used. Your findings in relation to your research questions are presented in the Results section. You should refrain from commenting on your results in this section and just simply present your findings. In the Discussion section, you should concisely summarize your findings, discuss how your results fit with what is already known in the field, and discuss the implications of your findings for practice and research.

71. Have experienced colleagues read your final manuscript for content, logic, and proofreading.

It is an excellent practice to have at least two colleagues provide feedback on your manuscript before sending it to the journal editor. Even more than grammar checking and punctuation, ask them to analyze the content and logic of the submission. Also, be sure to make the process of receiving the manuscript and providing feedback as simple as possible for them. For instance, ask if they prefer a hard copy or electronic, and how long they usually need to review an article for you. If possible, have the colleagues use the same criteria and form (if available) that the journal reviewers use to evaluate manuscripts.

72. Based on feedback (from your colleagues or the journal decision), consider your next steps in the manuscript revisions and submission process.

Once received by the journal editor, your article will be checked for compliance with author instructions and to make sure the topic is appropriate for the journal. If the article does not pass this initial screening, the editors return it to you usually with advice regarding whether to resubmit. For articles that make it past the initial screening, the review process usually takes several months. The decision you receive involves one of three possible scenarios: 1) acceptance with no changes, 2) conditional acceptance with revisions, or 3) rejection. If the editor invites you to revise and resubmit your article, do so as promptly as possible. Send your revised article with a letter detailing where each requested revision appears in the manuscript and explaining your reasoning for not complying with any suggested changes.

73. When at professional conferences, visit journal display tables and sessions.

Scanning the trends of publications for the last several years, there is a decided increase in the appearance of new journals across most fields every year. Contributors to this growing wave of opportunities include the continuing development of new areas of understanding and knowledge (consider nanotechnology, biopharmacology, technology changes' impact on education, etc.), and the reduced costs of publishing an online journal vs. paper based and postal delivered formats.

How do we stay current with all the new journal titles? Professional conferences are wonderful opportunities to learn about the publishing details of both familiar and new journals. Kathy makes it a habit to collect the fliers for the new journals in her research areas whenever she sees them. In this way, she builds a great range of publication possibilities for herself, students, and colleagues, and also has materials to provide faculty and students.

Category 7 Tips:

Writing Grants

74. Identify local, state, and federal sources of funding for your potential projects.

The first strategy we share with regard to writing grants is to identify potential sources of funding. For scholars, one of the main sources of grant funding is the government. Funding is available through state government agencies, such as state departments of education and labor, and through federal agencies, such as the National Science Foundation and the Institute of Education Sciences. Private foundations, as well as corporations, are also potential sources of funding. Searching the internet using specific key words related to your area of focus, geographic location, and organizational affiliation is a good way to start. In addition, your institution will likely have funding resources (including searchable foundation databases) and may even have trained personnel to assist you in identifying potential grant sources.

75. After identifying potential funding sources, serve as a proposal reviewer to better position yourself for future funding from these sponsors.

As a reviewer, you have the opportunity to work as part of a team, rating proposals according to specific criteria. Review panels convene either face-to-face at a designated site, or increasingly, meet online and conduct business virtually. Review panels are typically comprised of people with a range of grant experiences, giving you the opportunity to learn from your fellow panelists while seeing firsthand how successful and unsuccessful proposals are put together. In addition, service on review panels provides opportunities to interact and establish relationships with program officers from targeted funding agencies. In some cases service on review panels is strictly voluntary, but in others, such as with the US Department of Education, reviewers are paid a stipend for their service.

76. Review Requests for Proposals (RFP) from target agencies to determine the best fit with your background, expertise, and capacity.

Once target agencies and competitions have been identified, an important next step is to examine requests for proposals (RFPs) that fit the scope and time frame of your proposed project. Read the RFPs carefully to determine if you and your affiliated institution meet the qualification criteria. For example, if you work for an Institution of Higher Education (grant language for college or university) and the eligibility criteria specify that only local (LEA) and state education (SEA) agencies are eligible, then you would most likely not qualify to be the lead applicant or fiscal agent on the proposal. However, a partnership arrangement with an LEA or SEA might still be possible. Other questions to consider are:

- Is there enough time to complete and submit the application?
- What are the funding limits?
- Will the maximum amount allowed be enough to develop and deliver your project?
- Is there a realistic chance of being funded based on the number proposals to be funded?
- If funded, do you and your institution have the capacity to deliver the required activities proposed?

77. Identify target RFPs and request samples of the top funded proposals from prior competitions by the funding agency.

As soon as the specific RFP you will address is identified, it's a good idea to contact the program officer associated with the grant and ask for samples of top funded proposals from prior competitions. Private agencies and corporations will release these at their discretion, but publically funded entities such as state and federal government agencies are required to share this information, although there may be copy or mail costs.

78. Always carefully review and follow all agency guidelines and procedures for timely and appropriate submission and provide them to the appropriate institutional office.

Competition for grants is stiff. Funding agencies generally do not tolerate deviations from specified guidelines and often will not read proposals if applicants do not follow the procedures exactly. As reviewers, we have seen many proposals eliminated because applicants did not carefully adhere to page limits, acceptable font styles and sizes, required signatures, or submission deadlines. The point is to review the details and follow them! In addition, it is vital to consult your institution about submitting a grant in general and with specific details. They need to prepare to support you pre and post-award and process the application.

In addition, most agencies specify how to submit proposals. If electronic submission is required, it is important to register online with the funding agency in advance of the due date to establish login credentials and to become familiar with submission procedures. Very often, electronic submission systems will terminate your access after logging in if it is close to the deadline and multiple individuals are trying to submit simultaneously. Therefore, it is important to always submit at least one day in advance (allow at least one extra day in your timeline).

If the submission is by mail, it is critical to determine if the due date is the date the proposal must be received by the agency or if it is a postmark date. Also be sure to double check addresses. Agencies often specify different mail points for US postal deliveries and courier services such as Federal Express. Finally, if you plan to hand deliver your proposal, first check to see if this is an allowable option, and, if so, be sure to get an exact location, hours, and the phone number for a contact person. Be certain to obtain written verification that your grant was received on time when you deliver it.

79. Conduct research to gather data for the "Need" section of the proposal.

In the "Need" section of your proposal, you should succinctly state why there is a need for the project and what he grant will do specifically to address it. Assume that the funder knows something, but not everything, about your topic of concern. Your need statement should include current data and recent literature to support funding of your proposal. If the scope of your grant is broad, you will need to demonstrate that there is a need for the outcomes of your project beyond your local community. In demonstrating need for a wide reaching project, it is best to start with the overall need, which in many cases will be at a national level, and then move to demonstrating need at the state and local level.

80. Request "boilerplate" material from your institution to use in the institutional resource and capacity sections of the proposal.

Institutions typically maintain a professionally written narrative regarding the profile, resources, and capacity of the organization. This document is commonly referred to in grant language as a "boilerplate." You should request the boilerplate from your grants office or similar entity at your institution. Most will allow you to use the document freely and usually provide a Microsoft Word or similarly formatted version that you can modify according to your specific needs.

81. Draft sample and request letters of support for your proposal from potential grant partners or key organizations and individuals related to the specific RFP and project.

Carefully note the types and number of support letters allowed by the funding agency. In some instances, no number will be specified, but overall number of pages in the appendices, where the letters typically go, will be limited. Most funding agencies are not interested in receiving cheerleading letters from prominent individuals, but instead want letters from people who are familiar with the potential grantee's track record and who will have a relationship with the proposed project. For example, if you will be partnering with a community agency to assist you with participant referrals for your proposed project, the funding agency would expect to see a letter from the community group attesting to your work in the project area and specifying that if your proposal is funded, they plan to assist you with referrals. Contact potential partners, and if they agree to support your project, in the interest of time, offer to draft a sample letter for them or send "bullet points" with key information about the proposed project. Letter writers will add their own details, but most appreciate a starting template.

82. Identify and include deliverables and develop objectives, activities, and timeline in your proposal.

Carefully review the advisory language in the RFP to determine the funding agency's priorities and note activities that are allowed and whether there are any that are not permissible. If competitive priorities such as emphasis in certain areas or involvement with particular external groups are specified, determine if and how you will address these in your proposal. Succinctly state the overall goals of your project and describe how you will attain those goals. If deliverables are associated with the project, describe each deliverable, providing information regarding format, scope, and timeline. Specify measurable objectives that will allow you to reach your goals and delineate activities and a timeline for each objective.

83. Identify and include tables/charts listing key personnel and develop a management plan to help plan and implement your project.

Although several people may work on putting the proposal together, it is important to identify early in the development stage who will actually work on the project if it is funded. In particular, funding agencies will want to know the background and qualifications of key personnel including the proposed director. Abridged resumes or vitae highlighting relevant expertise for key personnel should be appended to the proposal. Funders also will expect a breakdown of how much time each person will devote to the project and a detailed management plan explaining how key personnel will work together to implement the grant.

84. Develop an evaluation plan aligned with objectives, activities, deliverables, and a timeline.

The first decision you will need to make regarding the evaluation plan is whether you will conduct the evaluation internally as part of your project, or instead hire an external evaluator. Funding agencies will often specify which they prefer, and may set a dollar or percentage of funding limit if you need to hire an external evaluator. If you decide to contract with an external evaluator, you can expect that they will provide major assistance in writing the evaluation section of the grant. They provide this service with the understanding that if the grant is funded, they will be paid to conduct the evaluation. On the other hand, if you propose to conduct the evaluation internally, you will need to write that section yourself. If you have clearly articulated your goals, deliverables, objectives, activities, and timeline, writing an evaluation plan should be fairly straightforward. You will need to specify the types of information you will collect, when you will collect it, and how you will analyze it to determine if you have met your proposal's goals and objectives.

85. Review your draft proposal using a "reviewer's guide" from the funding agency, or one you create based on the guidelines.

If the official Reviewer's Guide is not posted or included in your RFP, create a "reviewer's guide" for your proposal listing every criterion and sub-criterion from the RFP with a corresponding page number from your proposal. This will serve as a final checklist for you that proves you addressed all criterion, and it will clearly indicate to reviewers that you have addressed every criterion and make it easy for them to find the corresponding information in your proposal.

86. Have colleagues review your draft proposal and provide feedback.

Share a draft of your proposal with colleagues and ask them to provide feedback using the categories from the RFP and your reviewer's guide. You need to solicit feedback on both the proposal's content and readability. Serving as a "friendly reviewer" for colleagues' proposals provides an excellent opportunity for graduate students and junior faculty to build experience with the external funding process.

87. Develop the budget and circulate to your institution's key personnel for review and signatures.

The budget section of your grant provides a detailed breakdown of the costs associated with the proposed project. These costs will usually fall into the broad categories of direct and indirect costs. Direct costs are the actual expenses associated with the project such as personnel salaries and fringe benefits, travel, supplies, equipment, etc. Indirect costs are those that the grantee's institution charges to administer the grant. Funding agencies typically specify allowable and non-allowable expenses and often set limits on indirect cost amounts. A template divided into allowable budget categories is often included in the RFP. If they do not provide any, it is a good idea to review examples of funded grants from the target agency to see how successful proposers present their budgets.

Be careful not to overestimate your expenses or pad the budget. Your institution will probably have experienced staff who can guide you in planning your budget. Take advantage of this resource. Once your draft budget is complete, circulate it among key institutional personnel. Even if a supervisor's specific signature is not required, we advise securing it on a separate document to provide evidence that you contacted each level for approval. Several levels of administrators will need to sign off on the proposal. It is wise to contact them promptly and provide ample time for this process in order to avoid last minute delays in processing your proposal. We have colleagues who have missed deadlines because they expected university officials to approve and sign proposals in short periods.

88. Based on feedback from colleagues, revise and submit the proposal in accordance with institutional and agency policies.

Once you have reviewed suggestions from colleagues and revised your proposal accordingly, the final step is submission. If you are submitting the proposal yourself, be sure to follow all of the institutional and funding agency policies. Many institutions do not allow individual employees to submit grants directly to funding agencies, but instead handle all submissions through an authorized representative (AR). It is important that you identify this person early in the proposal development process and work closely with them or their staff to insure compliance with all institutional policies. You should also share a copy of the target RFP with the AR's staff so that they can become familiar with the agency's expectations for submission.

Category 8 Tips:

Writing Academic Books

89. Identify the need for a new publication in your area of expertise.

Based on your expertise and research, consider what new publication would benefit the field. It may be that presenting your research or expertise in a different or extended format could benefit the field greatly. Providing an in-depth presentation of extended research cannot be accomplished in single journal articles, but a book length discussion may be much more effective. In addition, the format of the proposed book could provide new contributions to the field. Review your book shelf and consider your favorite books: what format were they? Why were they successful? A list of such formats may include case studies, histories, autoethnographies, compilations, edited volumes, textbooks, and more.

90. Identify which valued publishers focus on your discipline.

Based on the ideas you developed above, consider which publishers best serve your areas of interest. You need to remember two critical points at this point: 1) not all publishers are interested in all types of publications, and 2) they are not all reputable. Publishers usually focus on serving specific disciplines because they have editors specializing in reviewing and guiding work in those fields, and an established reputation, recognition, and representation within them. Unlike novels written by best-selling authors, you will seldom receive a forward on your royalties, but neither will reputable academic publishers charge fees for publishing your work. For most people reading this volume, one of the goals in publishing a book is to enhance your academic vitae for tenure and promotion. Self-publishing, or vanity publishing, will not serve that purpose. Therefore, choosing an appropriate and well-respected publisher for your book will provide better recognition of your work, better credibility for it, and a better venue for distribution.

91. Review the authors' guidelines for book proposals for those publishers you are considering.

Just like when you write journal articles, you need to obtain the book proposal guidelines prior to crafting it. These are now usually through the publisher's website, but in some cases you might have to write a query letter to the acquisitions editor to request the guidelines. Once you have them, review the details and identify any sections which are unclear. Check the website and related materials for additional information; if none is found, tactfully contact the editors for clarity. Publisher booths or display tables at conferences may also have copies of these guidelines.

92. When you attend professional conferences, visit the book editors of identified publishers to discuss interest, requirements, and process.

In some cases, it is helpful to develop a relationship with publishers, an opportunity you can often find at professional conferences. As you visit the publisher booths, be sure to identify yourself as a prospective author, not a book purchaser, so that you will be directed to the correct people. Sometimes they do not attend conferences, but you will likely be able to obtain a business card for the specific person related to your discipline. If you do not have opportunity to meet with an editor at the conference, browse the books on display to determine if this will indeed be a good venue for your book.

93. Complete every book proposal for the specific publisher. (Be sure to fulfill the specific guidelines completely.)

Follow the book proposal guidelines completely. One easy way to accomplish this goal is to use the headings of the required sections as the headings for your proposal. This simple approach enables the editors to find the essential elements they need quickly for their decision. Moreover, when the guidelines request specific details such as purpose, audience, comparison of competing books, be sure to provide thorough but concise responses. As editors and reviewers, we find this to be a common failure with proposals- incomplete fulfillment of the guidelines.

94. Review the book contract carefully, consult a literary lawyer if you have detailed questions.

When you receive the good news that the publisher would like to publish your book, you will receive a contract. Like all legal documents, it is important that you read the contract fully and closely. Literary contracts are not much like anything most professors encounter in other contexts; therefore, we recommend contacting a literary lawyer to assist in interpreting the document. What is at stake? In most cases, literary contracts assign all rights of the publication to the publisher with a small-percentage royalty allocated to academic authors. While the royalty may seem like the greatest concern; however, the electronic, video, film, and translation and international rights or controls could be of equal importance. Understanding the greater scope of consideration makes the need for a literary lawyer's review clearer.

95. There are many items that need to be included in contracts which authors might think are standard, but for which various publishers charge additional fees.

As you discuss pre-production, production, and post-production requirements, responsibilities, and specifics, be sure to detail you expectations and needs with the publisher. For instance, while some publishers charge the academic author for creating a book index, a few still include it as a matter of course. Others provide free copies to all book authors or contributors; however, more frequently this practice is disappearing. Consider who pays for and distributes review copies for journals, who provides fliers for conferences, your cost for author copies of the book, who is responsible for reprinting if major errors are found after production, and whether there are any additional costs for marketing the book in any of your desired venues, journals, or conferences. These are just a few of the areas we see authors encounter unpleasant surprises post contract signing. The varied list illustrates the wide variety of topics and the need for specialized legal counsel to review your contract.

96. Identify page counts for each chapter and section of chapter to guide your writing efforts.

Before commencing writing, we suggest retrieving the outline you submitted with your book proposal and planning your page count. This strategy includes identifying the number of pages you anticipate for each chapter and then section of the book. This approach has several benefits: 1) it breaks the overwhelming writing task into small segments, 2) it helps you plan the realistic amount of space available for each section, and 3) it provides more achievable short-term goals. Give the page count strategy a try and see how it increases your productivity.

97. Continue to refer to the outline as you develop each chapter of the book to maintain focus.

In the book proposal, you had to include an outline; this outline will be a great aid for you in your book development. Most people do not think that using an outline is important, but in fact, when writing a book, you need one more than ever. An outline has many benefits, including keeping your writing focused, ensuring the completeness of your content, and guiding logical progression of thought. However, the outline should not strangle your work; even when you use it as a guide, it can also be changed to allow for missing elements, additions, and more depth. Therefore, when you see something that needs to be added or deleted, make edits to your outline and continue. The outline guides and supports your creativity, but should never nullify it.

98. Insert citations and references as you write without disrupting the flow of you work, but maintain the accuracy of your records.

We find that we avoid a great deal of work if we insert citations and references as we write our large manuscripts. When writing, sometimes we cannot recall the exact citation, but we can insert a placeholder and mark it with a highlight color to complete later. However, when we do know the citations, we insert them and open the reference page to insert an entry for the item as well. Again, we might not have the entire reference handy, but compiling the list will speed along the final editing and citation-reference reconciliation.

99. Be certain to address diversity and cross-cultural considerations in the examples, names, and language used in your book.

We discussed earlier in the book a commitment to cross-cultural communication and sensitivity. This commitment also applies to our writing. Think about how you feel when you read a book with examples that do not reflect your profession or culture. It increases your distance from the author and the book. You can take specific steps to avoid doing the same to your readers. One strategy is to plan your examples, scenarios, cases, etc., so that they include people of different race, gender, education, socioeconomic status or class, religion, and nationality. Sometimes, only their name reveals their identity; however, it will be a sufficient indicator for those who need to envision themselves in the examples.

100. Request that a few colleagues read the final draft and provide feedback prior to submission to the editor.

Just as we suggest for journal article manuscripts and conference submissions, leverage the wealth of insight ad experience you share with your colleagues. When you request that they review/provide feedback for one of your books, be sure to offer a compensatory professional service. You might also ask some leaders in your field to review the book prior to publication to not only help mold the final edits, but also offer recommendations which, with their permission, may appear on the back cover of the published work.

101. Consider the editorial and any other reviews as professional recommendations, while holding to your purpose, ethics, and convictions.

This section's final tip is seldom discussed in academic circles, but much needed. Sometimes editors or publishers will have in their minds' what they believe your book should look or read like. Sometimes we discover through conversation that their recommendations are well-grounded, valid, and needed. However, occasionally the differences between our expertise in the discipline and their current role, usually further removed from active research, leads to a disagreement about content or format.

In these cases, we encourage you to seek advice from a trusted and experienced colleague. However, please know you might have to part ways with your original publisher. This severance can occur if you believe requested changes compromise your research findings, professional ethics, or convictions. In these cases, although both parties signed the original contract, sometimes they cannot reach an agreement about publishing or content particulars. However, even though you may feel the situation is urgent, we would suggest having another publisher in the wings before nullifying the first contract. These are the sort of stressful situations that make having well-established relationships with publishers and editors helpful. In cases when professionals respect one another, they can agree to disagree and perhaps work together in the future.

Category 9 Tips:

Ethics and Responsibility

102. Become familiar with FERPA regulations; complete training if available at your institution.

The Family Educational Rights and Privacy Act (FERPA) is a federal law enacted to protect the privacy of students' educational records. Your institution will most likely have either online or face-to-face training on the law's implementation and your responsibilities related to it. Take advantage of this training to ensure that students' rights are protected and to avoid legal issues. Be assured that claiming ignorance of legal requirements is never a valid defense. Moreover, in the current litigious climate, FERPA is very important for faculty, higher education institutions, and students. Even if other faculty might tell you not to worry about this issue, pursue training and follow the guidelines to sustain a successful career as a scholar.

103. Research your discipline's professional associations and licensing requirements (if applicable) to determine the specific code of ethics.

Most professional associations, as well as professional licensing bodies, have their own codes of ethics. It is important to adhere to these from the very beginning of your professional career. Review your professional association's website for information regarding their specific code of ethics. If none of your associations have a code of ethics, find a closely related field to provide direction. Codes related to professional licenses can usually be found on your state's licensure board's website under codes or standards of professional practice.

104. Become familiar with the Acceptable Use Policy (AUP) or internet policy at your institution and organizations to

determine what is acceptable use of institutional resources and equipment.

Your institution will most likely have an Acceptable Use Policy (AUP) consisting of rules that specify how you may and may not use resources such as the institution's computer network, e-mail system, and equipment. You should become familiar with the policy and understand that you are personally responsible if it is violated. Moreover, most institutions have strict policies about not using organizational equipment and resources for personal or outside use. In other words, do not make copies for your local nonprofit at your school, or conduct a consulting business via your institutional email account or telephone. Regarding security issues, it is important that you keep your network login and email password information private. Equipment and room keys belonging to your institution should never be shared with other employees, students, or outsiders.

105. Become familiar with traditional and digital copyright laws for educational Fair Use, publication, and internet postings.

The opportunity to use other authors' published material, as well as to widely disseminate your own ideas, is essential to your work as a scholar. At the same time, protection of the intellectual property of all parties is critical. Many professionals' careers have been destroyed due to plagiarism that may have seemed minor at the time. The easy availability of copyrighted material via the internet makes balancing the desire for access to a wide range of material with the need to safeguard intellectual property increasingly challenging. A helpful guideline is to paraphrase content you read and cite the original source. Supporting this practice includes keeping efficient and easily retrievable reference records. You may obtain personal, field/discipline specific assistance in understanding how to legally access and use copyrighted material in your teaching and scholarly writing from your institution's library. Moreover, Fair Use of copyrighted material continues to change with the digital age. It is misleading to believe you have great latitude with educational use of copyrighted material, because in many cases these rules do not apply to online materials and online course spaces (BlackBoard, Moodle, etc.) Your library support and general counsel personnel are good sources of information and support regarding these issues.

106. Avoid even the appearance of plagiarism by always fully citing sources and checking work in plagiarism identification software before submission.

Issues related to plagiarism are potentially among the most serious threats to the academic reputation of emerging scholars. There is no acceptable excuse for deliberately passing off someone else's work as your own. While this is common knowledge among scholars and easily prevented, avoiding involvement with more subtle forms of plagiarism and even the appearance of plagiarism, involves careful attention to citation of sources and double-checking work in plagiarism identification software before submission (i.e., Turnitin.com, Checkforplagiarism.net, etc.). You should take advantage of your institution's resources in this area. Your library will most likely have the software available, as well as online tutorials you can access to brush up on things you need to keep in mind for avoiding plagiarism.

107. Become familiar with the human subjects protection policies.

In response to the widespread and often tragic abuse of human subjects in research (Beecher 1966) that has historically taken place, institutions now adhere strongly to codes of ethics in research that includes provisions for the protection of human subjects. These protective measures are monitored closely by Institutional Review Boards (IRB's), which review research proposals to ensure that they include safeguards for the protection of human subjects. It is important to understand that you cannot conduct any research involving human subjects without first gaining approval through your IRB, and often also obtaining informed consent from your research participants. Your institution might have required training that you need to complete prior to applying for IRB approval for your research or grant work; therefore, it is better to research this area and determine what is needed early in your research agenda construction.

108. Review institutional policies and procedures regarding conflict of interest.

Conflicts of interest arise when actions related to your professional responsibilities are compromised by your personal interests or other professional roles (i.e., hiring your daughter on your grant project, contracting for services with a company in which you are part owner, etc.). Your institution will most likely have a policies specifying the need to disclose any potential conflicts of interest and directing you to avoid situations that could cause observers to question your ability to objectively fulfill your professional responsibilities. Trust is a critical component of a scholar's work. You should closely adhere to these policies and be careful to avoid situations that could be perceived as potential conflicts of interest.

109. Review faculty handbook policies and procedures regarding interactions with colleagues and students.

As with conflicts of interest, actions that could be perceived as potentially undermining your ability to behave objectively and fairly with regard to colleagues and students should be avoided. Your institution will likely have specific policies addressing consensual relationships between individuals with different degrees of power, such as between deans and faculty or faculty and students. Romantic or sexual relationships in these circumstances, even when consensual, may be cause for reprimand or termination of employment.

110. Review institutional policies and procedures regarding travel requirements, reimbursements, and limitations.

Professional travel reimbursements and arrangements include many specific stipulations that you need to learn and follow in detail. Our strongest advice is to allow plenty of time to process your travel request and learn the rules prior to making any travel plans. In many cases, your institution will provide funding to cover some or all of your expenses when traveling as part of your professional development and responsibilities as a scholar.

111. Follow strategies to ensure compliance with travel requirements, reimbursements, and limitations.

The following are five steps to guide you in learning and complying with stipulations related to travel requirements, reimbursements, and limitations. The first step is to find out up front how much money you have for travel for the year and plan accordingly. Secondly, since most organizations have travel policies and procedures that must be strictly adhered to for reimbursement in order to prevent abuse of institutional travel fund, you need to learn the rules governing travel before making plans. Your institution's website or employee handbook should have travel guidelines readily available. If not, inquire through your supervisor or company HR division. Thirdly, most institutions require written authorization before travel arrangements may be booked (hotel reservations, flights, conference registration); therefore, advanced planning is critical. Fourthly, you will need to find out if there are limits on hotel and airline costs, as well as whether the actual cost of meals will be reimbursed or if you will get a set rate per day (per diem). Also, keep in mind that most employers limit the use of rental cars and often specify the size of cars that can be rented, if allowed. Coverage of incidental expenses such as taxi fares, hotel internet charges, tips and airport parking will also need to be factored into your planning. Not all institutions will cover these expenses and it is better to know in advance. Fifthly, the source of your funding (i.e., grant, department, college, etc.) will usually determine additional factors for allowed and disallowed items and limits.

112. Review institutional policies and procedures for purchases, finances, budgets, and reimbursements.

Although most emerging scholars have had little or no formal training in financial management, many find themselves facing greater responsibility than ever for monetary matters as pressure for external funding increases and reductions in support staff continue. Compliance with institutional policies and procedures regarding financial matters is critical in avoiding serious legal and ethical issues that could threaten your career and result in legal action against you. For example, many institutions have strict policies and detailed procedures regarding the collection, storage, and disbursement of cash for any purpose. For example, a naïve scholar might innocently assume that it's okay to charge fees to participants to cover the cost of a workshop as long as there is no profit. However, this type of action is definitely something that could lead to serious ethical dilemmas and legal trouble if it violates institutional policies or procedures. Your institution's controller's office should have policies and procedures available and perhaps posted on their website. In some colleges, the controllers' office may also have tutorials to assist you in becoming familiar with the specific details. Taking advantage of these resources early on will help you avoid problems later, especially at times when you may be working under tight deadlines and rushing to get things done.

113. Identify examples of research ethical conflicts from The Chronicle of Higher Education or professional journals; consider consequences and alternative proactive approaches.

One way to become familiar with potential situations that could cause ethical dilemmas is to review past issues of publications like the Chronicle of Higher Education, which provides weekly accounts of happenings in academe. The Chronicle frequently includes tales of ethical misconduct along with readers' comments, which can be helpful in examining these often complex issues from multiple perspectives. Take the time to research and review published accounts of ethical issues affecting scholars. Consider the course of action taken in the cases presented and how to avoid the negative outcomes. Ask yourself or discuss with colleagues how to avoid the situation itself and what your institution's response would have been. Most of all, identify proactive strategies to recognize such potential conflicts and avoid them.

114. Build knowledge by attending a seminar or session on professional ethics at a professional conference.

Scholars can quickly find themselves confronted by a wide range of ethical dilemmas. Attendance at seminars sponsored by professional organizations in your field and ethics focused sessions at local, state, and national conferences can assist you in becoming familiar with ethical guidelines specific to your discipline and to the higher education environment. In addition, these sessions are an excellent opportunity to interact with others in your field and gain insight into their perspectives on common ethical challenges. A few organizations that provide different insights on issues of ethics in higher education include the American College Personnel Association (ACPA) - College Student Educators International, the American Psychological Association (APA), the American Educational Research Association (AERA), the American Philosophical Association (APA), and the National Association of College and University Business Officers (NACUBO).

115. Identify "hot topics" in ethics and related recommendations for your discipline.

As academics, we must consider not only our roles as educators in our institutions, but also as researchers, authors, and experts in our disciplines. What ethical issues arise in each of these areas for our specific discipline and context? Clear illustrations of the differences in ethical issues emerge in the IRB requirements for historical research (perhaps in liberal arts, or social sciences) compared to medical research with human subjects. In another example, the release of startling or alarming findings of economic or political research might have far-reaching ethical considerations. How have others in your discipline handled these issues in the past? What have been the positive and negative outcomes of their actions? These are important topics to investigate and discuss with colleagues as one develops as an academic.

Category 10 Tips:

Technology for Writing and Teaching

116. As professionals, we need to employ Netiquette in all electronic communications; the potential damage and risks are too great not to be vigilant in this area.

Online communications can greatly aid our efficiency with colleagues and students; they can also broaden our professional network to global dimensions and be indispensable for collaborative efforts. However, we need to conduct our electronic communications with our professional conduct and responsibilities firmly in mind. No doubt you can list several faculty, administrators, or other professionals who have been humiliated and/or lost their jobs because of poor judgment in their electronic communications. Netiquette encompasses the appropriate use of etiquette in technology and internet contexts. While we do not have an Emily Post to set the standard of netiquette, common sense, respect for others, professional behavior, and courtesy provide substantial guidelines for discerning appropriate choices.

Specific concerns for online communications include conventions which people new to online communications may be unaware. Such conventions, and in some cases requirements, include:

1. Not using work email for personal communications
2. Never using all capital letters in postings or emails (it is the equivalent to yelling)
3. Being sure to use relevant subject headings in email
4. Not reacting in anger to someone's communication (flaming)

5. Not putting anything in online writing that you don't want to see on a public billboard or nightly newscast
6. Not emailing personal responses to entire email lists or groups
7. Always spell checking your messages
8. Not using chat acronyms in professional correspondence

While some of items seem common sense, others are a function of the fact that most emails and online posts may never be deleted. Additionally, even if they are deleted, there are ways to retrieve them if needed (i.e., legal action). The conundrum with professional risk and electronic communication is that we need to respond frequently and rapidly in this media. Yet our advice is to consider the guidelines listed above and always re-read your reply/post prior to submission.

117. Learn how to access your institution's complete online library resources efficiently.

When we think back to the physical version of the card catalog, few services in higher education have changed as drastically as library access and resources (i.e., you may need to use an additional login access or different URL). Therefore, this area remains one in which faculty need to seek new information, support, and training. For instance, accessing and reading library content from your campus office is likely achieved in a very different manner than from off-campus. Moreover, the growing number of tools and resources available through our libraries continues to grow. We cannot emphasize enough the value of building a good relationship with the librarian(s) assigned to your department or discipline. Their role is to keep current with the newest developments and offerings for library resources in your field and to support faculty in learning how to use them, yet few faculty access librarians (information specialists) and their skills for this purpose. From new statistical databases, to e-books, citation linkers, and inter-library loan, the resources we have access to continue to grow, yet we may be unaware of what is available, and how to access and use it. In addition, you might not realize how much library content can be linked into your learning management system for your courses. We recommend sending an email to your designated librarian asking for her suggestions in these areas. We are certain you will increase the breadth of materials you have access to and increase your literary research efficiency.

118. Use an online reference database management system to store, retrieve, and organize your academic citations and references.

Refworks™ and Endnote™ are major examples of online and stand-alone reference database management systems that can change the way you develop your reference lists. The basic way that such tools work is that you input or import your reference document citations/records into the program and they become part of a personal reference database. When you write papers and books, you can search for those citations you cannot quite remember; you can also insert citations and references directly from the database and not have to retype them repeatedly. While we find you still need to check the format style (e.g., APA, MLA, etc.) for details, this tool can greatly streamline your referencing work. Be certain to contact your institution's IT department and library prior to purchasing such products, as they may provide licenses already, as well as training or tutorials available.

119. Use a virtual drive to store and access your files from any location that has internet access.

Are you working at the office and need a file on your home computer? Frustrating, isn't it? Do you forget which computer you stored your current work on—i.e., desktop, laptop, or tablet? Virtual drives can change your life as a faculty member and increase your productivity greatly. Using "cloud computing," many companies provide a substantial amount of free space with high reliability by linking servers through the web. The emergent favorite is Dropbox.com.

How do these virtual drives work? You sign up for a free account, create folders in which to store your files, upload them, and voilà, you are in action. Either you can log in over the website to access your files, or you can download the free application which installs the drive on your computer. Using the latter makes using Dropbox.com seem like you are just saving to another hard drive. You retrieve from and save to that folder on your computer and then the program synchronizes the contents with your virtual drive. Be ready to save time and reduce frustration!

120. Explore how online resources such as Google Docs, Dropbox, and others can facilitate greater productivity in collaborative writing projects.

When working with colleagues on collaborative writing projects, it is always a challenge to identify whether you have the latest, most up to date, version of a file. We solve this frustrating issue by using virtual shared folders.

What this means is that:

1. The co-authors decide which free or paid online service they would like to use for the specific project
2. One author uploads all the current files he or she has for the project to a designated folder
3. This author now shares the folder with the colleague by sending a system "invitation" (usually you just insert the recipient's email address)
4. The other author accepts the invitation and sets up a free user account of their own
5. Now they both can access the files, make edits, and add and delete files

The major benefit is that when either user opens the virtual folder they always have access to the most recent work!

The two examples of Google Docs and Dropbox have different strengths. Google Docs is helpful because it has the editing programs included (e.g., word processor, spreadsheet, etc.), and allows multiple people to work on a file simultaneously. A limitation of Google Docs is that files can lose their formatting (i.e., tables, figures, etc). Dropbox is another viable option, and does not lose file formatting. However, with Dropbox you need to have your application (i.e., word processor, etc.) on the computer you use to create and edit the files.

121. Explore the many benefits of using remote computer access.

There are many times when remote computing could be of great assistance to professors, but they are not familiar enough with the benefits to take advantage of the solution. Presently, there are several free and paid remote access solutions, which allow one to login to a computer in another location and, in some cases, not only access files, but also use the programs, as well as peripherals (e.g., printer, plotter, etc.). You might be familiar with this capability if a computer technician has logged into your computer to make a repair, configure a program, or demonstrate how to use a program.

You can use these and more functions by simply downloading or accessing a remote access program. Why might these programs be helpful for professors and scholars? Consider the following applications for our roles: 1) accessing files on our home or office computer without having to travel back to the location, 2) using programs on your remote computer, which you do not have on the computer you have available locally (high end data analysis software, graphic design, specialized software, etc.), 3) demonstrating software or solutions to a student or colleague one on one, and 4) accessing hardware devices that are connected to the remote computer. Moreover, there are many more possibilities that you will discover.

These remote access programs are more user friendly for the novice and intermediate user than ever before. Consider installing one of the following products on a trial basis to determine which meets your needs best. Enjoy discovering the many ways remote access will benefit your productivity and decrease frustration! Please note some of these services/programs never charge a fee for basic features, while others may have a monthly fee. Best bets for remote access computing include: Logmein.com, GoToMyPc.com, RemotePC.Com, VNC, Microsoft Remote Access computing (part of Windows Vista and later), TeamViewer.com, and AnyPlace-Control.com.

122. Establish and use backup procedures frequently and regularly.

Okay, we all know we should, but few of us actually do employ backup procedures as often as we should. It is somewhat like flossing your teeth; no one wants to bother until there is a problem! However, once most academics lose a few years worth of data, curriculum, and papers to a lightning storm, a hard drive failure, or dastardly computer infection, they usually begin to consider the urgency of routine backups more seriously.

There are many options for backup routines, which range from free to expensive. First, your institution may provide capability for backups to be set up and then activated transparently for you; check with IT first.

However, beware: usually these services will only apply to your office computer. Therefore, you may still need to determine how to backup your computers at home or other locations. Second, look online for a free backup system that you can configure to backup automatically in the background while your computer is online. (A reliable example of this sort is MozyBackup.com). Third are hardware options, which range from external to internal drives and USB drives. One of the drawbacks of external drives is that if an electrical disturbance strikes your location, the external drive will fail also! In addition, if your computer is stolen, the thieves will also likely take the drive that is sitting next to it. The internal drives are usually in the format of a RAID system, which functions as simultaneous mirror. They are automatic, and transparent to your activity; however, again, if someone steals the computer, or the electricity spikes, they too will be useless. Consider a combination of hardware and online solutions. Set them up to function without user intervention, and then check every few months to make sure they are still working. You will not be in dire panic the next time your main drive fails.

123. Identify assistive technology and ergonomic considerations for yourself, collaborators, and students.

As an academic in the 21st century, you use a lot technology every day. Because the pervading culture of the USA does not emphasize ergonomic adjustments for computer and technology use, we are especially susceptible to related physical difficulties (e.g., carpal tunnel syndrome, Repetitive Stress Injury (RSI), back pain, neck pain, vision changes, etc.). Add to this the fact that we are an aging population and one realizes why visual and hearing deficits, joint pain, and back pain often arise. Kathy, like many HEI professors and staff members, has had severe back problems and RSI. Therefore, addressing these issues has been essential for her to continue to work. The great news is that more technology solutions emerge every year, providing alternatives that reduce pain and damage to our bodies. For instance, computers built after 2008 include several free software tools such as screen magnifiers (to enlarge the screen), voice recognition (to decrease the amount of typing needed), and screen readers (to reduce the amount of reading required) (King 2011). Moreover, identifying the proper posture and alignment for computer use will reduce pain and additional damage. We list several web sites below to provide guidance on this topic.

Even if you do not currently feel pain in your back, neck, or shoulders, be proactive and learn how to prevent them. In addition, awareness of assistive technology options provides valuable information to evaluate options for the class work you provide and provide information for students with these needs.

What is ergonomics? (video presentation):

http://www.butterscotch.com/tutorial/What-Is-Ergonomics-

Ergonomics and Positioning tutorial:

http://www.customtyping.com/tutorials/erg/ergonomics.htm

M Healthy website:

http://hr.umich.edu/mhealthy/programs/ergonomics/help.html

124. Learn how to use the online learning management system used at your institution for teaching all classes.

Whether you teach classes in face to face, traditional, online, or hybrid contexts, it is essential to learn your institution's learning management system (LMS). A LMS is an online platform that provides space to post documents, presentations, etc., facilitate online discussions, receive student uploads of assignments, store and deliver class materials to students, maintain a grade book, provide student feedback, and more. By now, you might be thinking of your HEI's LMS; it is most likely Blackboard™, Moodle, Sakai, Angel, WebCT/Blackboard™, OpenUSS, or another.

Why would faculty use a LMS for a face to face class? Because it offers the ability to manage the class and distribute materials much more efficiently. Instead of emailing documents repeatedly through the semester, or killing countless trees through printing, you can post them in the online space and the students retrieve them as needed. We set up a class in the LMS system once and let the students retrieve what they needed, when they needed it. A second important benefit of LMS systems includes building greater student responsibility for learning as they retrieve information, engage in peer discussion, and potentially offer content suggestions. The final benefit mentioned in our limited space is the cultivation of twenty-first century learning skills though the LMS experience. Students will use technology platforms and communicate via technology in their future careers, so by using them in our classes, we prepare them to understand the strengths and weaknesses of these communication modes, as well as master their communication and technical skills in context. If you hesitate to use a LMS because of lack of experience or understanding, seek out support services your HEI provides. As we address our learning challenges, we model for our students the courage to learn.

125. Learn and determine which instructional technologies will benefit student learning in your courses.

New hardware and software that can be used effectively in instructional settings emerge at a breakneck speed. However, most faculty are not experts in instructional technology. Since the 1980s, HEIs have added instructional designers and faculty developers to address these faculty learning needs. Whether you need to use the document camera, smart board, LCD projector, or lecture capture products, identify one or two to investigate per year and meet with the instructional technology staff to determine how to use and apply them to your teaching. While it takes time, and yes may include risk of error, there are several benefits to investing this effort: increasing your teaching efficiency, improving student engagement, including different learning styles in your classes, and incorporating current content. King and Cox (2011) provide faculty direction in "taming technology" with a book that provides a quick overview of why and how to use different technologies in teaching. This book also provides steps and strategies to begin learning and applying them.

126. Learn and incorporate Universal Design Instruction (UDI).

Consistent with several of the prior tips in this section, we recommend learning more about and finding ways to incorporate UDI. UDI refers to improving teaching and learning so that all people learn better (Scott, McGuire, and Shaw 2001). As they design their course content, instructional plan, and assignments, the model guides faculty to consider varied learning styles, learning preferences, and learning, physical, or other disabilities. DO-IT (Burgstahler 2011a) shares the seven UDI principles and straightforward recommendations for implementation. Funded by a federal grant in the 1990s, this project provides straightforward direction for addressing the needs of all learners in your classes (Burgstahler 2011a; 2011b; Burgstahler and Cory 2008). UDI helps us as faculty realize that people have different learning strengths and limitations, and by maximizing the variety of communication modes (e.g., audio, video, captions, scripts) and assignments (e.g., student created content, papers, presentations, group projects, etc.) we allow all students to reach their greatest capacity for participation and learning.

127. Audio or video record your class and conference presentations to improve your skills and develop instructional materials.

How many of us seek ways to increase our productivity without adding more work to our schedule? This tip is for all of you who want to accomplish this goal. Purchase or borrow a high quality audio or video digital recorder and tripod. Set it up to the side of the classroom next time you teach face to face and record ONLY you. Recording the sessions only takes about three minutes to set up and will not interfere with your class. However, you can use the recordings for several worthwhile benefits. First, view the videos much like football or golf training films: review, privately analyze, and learn from your best and worse teaching and facilitation interactions. Secondly, consider whether you might extract sections of the recordings to use as independent segments for student review, tutorials, or other instructional support. In all of our courses, there are difficult concepts that you have to explain several times. If you record those, clip them as separate 3-8 minute segments, and post them online in your password protected online space (or LMS), where students can view/listen to them multiple times, twenty-four hours a day, seven days a week. We like to think of this as teaching while we are sleeping! Not a bad concept: we maintain our usual schedule, and provide 24-7 resources for student night birds!

128. Improve your efficiency and teaching by developing brief, on-demand tutorials for critical topics or assignments.

In efforts to streamline and improve student support, Kathy has found that developing on-demand tutorials for college students is invaluable. When we swiftly develop tutorials and reviews, which students can access 24-7, the benefits for learning and development skyrocket. First, students can master content outside of class time at their own pace. Second, class time can focus on deeper content and application of the topics. One recommendation is not to develop highly technical tutorials, but instead brief screen-capture tutorials, narrated PowerPoint™ presentations, or video or audio lectures recorded with a webcam or USB microphone.

In this case, simple development and design are benefits for both faculty and students. Faculty may create all of these examples with free software usually available at HEIs. Again, once you create the tutorials, uploading them into your web learning platform will provide remote, anytime, and password-protected access. King and Cox (2011) provide direction for creating such custom instructional materials such as selecting among technology and format choices, writing brief scripts and keeping content to three to eight minutes for each tutorial.

129. Use virtual office hours and virtual meetings to facilitate communication and save time.

Of course, with our lives filled with so many meetings and responsibilities, it is often difficult to have time to collaborate or meet with students as much as we would like. At times it is plainly impossible to meet in person. For instance, using virtual platforms to collaborate, Kathy has co-authored many books with colleagues who live across the country or world, and Ann has worked with several doctoral students at a distance to finish their dissertations. Moreover, many faculty who teach online and face to face use virtual hours to meet with individual students more conveniently. Important benefits of virtual office hours are greater flexibility in scheduling, no travel time or cost, and the capacity to record the written or audio conversation for future reference.

We believe one needs to choose virtual meetings technologies with which people feel most comfortable; therefore, consider the range of options that can introduce and acclimate your colleagues and students to the benefits of virtual sessions. The following types of technologies are examples of those which fit different situations and needs:

1. Free conference calls (voice only) (e.g., Freeconference call.com, Skype and Google Voice are simple solutions)
2. Video conferencing (e.g., Skype, [illegible], [illegible].com, etc.)
3. Voice conferencing and desktop sharing (e.g., Skype, DimDim, etc.).

Category 11 Tips:

Passing It On: Mentoring Other Scholars

130. Identify colleagues for collaboration based on their related or complementary academic interests, expertise, and excellence.

We find that not everyone is in the habit of thinking about research interest connections among colleagues, and therefore they miss wonderful opportunities to expand their thinking, work, and professional development. Synergy is a fitting word to describe the excitement and productivity that emerges when you discover a good fit with a colleague related to research, publication, teaching, or service.

One of our themes in this book has been academic professionals as lifelong learners. Who else is more capable of supporting this goal than our colleagues? In creative and productive collaborations, there can be honest discussions and debates that stretch our perspective and ways of thinking beyond our isolated frames. Sometimes the most beneficial collaborations in respect to mutual growth include collaborating with colleagues from different disciplines. We strongly suggest you enjoy academic "cross fertilization" to stimulate new ways of examining familiar issues, building creative solutions, and exploring new possibilities.

131. Identify student mentees based on their excellent performance, initiative, and commitment to their professional growth, as well as the similarity of their academic interests to yours.

One of the results of cultivating a co-learning relationship with mentees is that mentors may gain fresh insights and energy for their own work. When many mentees seek your support, one way to facilitate this dynamic of both parties learning and growing is to work in similar fields. In this manner, not only will you be able to provide guidance related to professional and content areas, but also both parties experience validation and respect. Such professional relationships also model healthy collaborations with future colleagues for the mentee.

132. Share your vision of lifelong learning as an academic with potential collaborators to confirm similar focus and commitment.

For academics, our vision of lifelong learning within our profession is very much a core value. Just as we develop a philosophy of education to describe our teaching approach to colleagues and future employers, our understanding of lifelong learning in the academic life effectively describes our perspective and commitments. As you consider working with other scholars on extended research or writing projects, understanding their commitment to continuing professional learning reveals their intrinsic motivations.

These motivations will be instrumental when deadlines conflict with other demands, responsibilities, and pressures. For instance, will your colleagues commit extra time and effort to overcome barriers during the project? Is their investment limited to pride or recognition, or are they deeply committed to the purpose, topic, and outcomes of the effort? It is much more efficient and pleasant to work with people who share similar focus and commitment to their continuing development.

133. Share the stories of your academic journey to determine similar and/or complementary points upon which to build a collaborative relationship.

Understanding the academic history and journey of our colleagues provides another dimension of sharing perspectives, expectations, and decision making patterns. In the process, you also discover related interests, skills, and experiences that may inform projects or writing opportunities. In addition, the additional background provides the basis for a more informed decision about collaboration compatibility.

134. Discuss and establish the means for fairly representing everyone's contributions through authorship of all work.

Most professional associations and publication manuals have strict statements regarding attribution of authorship, and for good reason. The order in which authors need to be listed should reflect the effort and contribution to the manuscript. Based on this stipulation, any other approach is deceitful. However, a legitimate issue arises when co-authors contribute equally. In this case, rotating first authors on publications addresses the concern.

Another issue related to authorship emerges when some senior faculty never allow junior faculty or students to be first author on publications. Once gaining tenure and full professor, we have a great gift to offer to junior colleagues. In our collaborative work we can support their professional growth, but we can also encourage them to be first author when they do the substantial work. Be cautious to discern when students or colleagues are afraid to speak up for first author rights, because of power issues, or the (usually false) perception that submissions will receive better reviews if the senior person is listed first. Address these concerns and together make the choice that provides clarity and benefit.

135. Identify common research and projects that will be mutually beneficial to both parties.

In building your research and publishing agenda, do not lose sight of the fact that you want to invest your individual efforts in collaborative projects that will advance them. In practical terms, this means not becoming side-tracked with good, but not excellent, choices. In the process of developing collaborations with colleagues, discuss the potential mutual benefits available from working together. If the project mostly benefits one person, then issues of power, lack of motivation, or resentment may easily arise. Identifying research and publication efforts that mutually advance all parties have a much greater likelihood of success and satisfaction.

136. Develop provisional plans for the first project you will undertake together.

Before fully committing to your first project together with a new collaborator, why not consider outlining it's plans provisionally, or tentatively. In this manner, conversations can continue, more of the true shape of the project is free to emerge, and everyone involved can make a better informed decision about their commitment and potential risk in the project. By identifying the first round or two of plans as provisional, everyone should understand that the parties have not yet fully committed and that deciding not to continue is entirely acceptable. Using this strategy reduces pressure on all parties and allows people to walk away from projects early in the process without harm or embarrassment to anyone.

137. Address potential power issues before and during the collaboration.

Honest communication is critical to build excellent collaborations. Major reasons to cultivate excellent communication are that the imbalance of power in professional working relationships is both tricky and potentially damaging. While the next tips will address some specifics on this issue of power, the overall principle is that when one member of the collaborative has supervisory or decision-making power over another, then it is difficult for the subordinate to freely voice opinions and needs. In the academy, junior colleagues need to evaluate carefully the risks of working on research and publishing projects with faculty who will vote on their tenure and promotion application. As an example, we recall several situations where senior faculty demanded first authorship, extra grant stipends, or slacked off on their commitment when working with pre-tenure faculty. In these situations, the imbalance of power makes it potentially dangerous/costly for junior colleagues to assert their rights. The best strategy is to carefully evaluate the culture of your organization, and watch the behavior of the colleague with whom you intend to work. Only then should one advance with the collaboration and discuss issues of equal division of labor, recognition, and compensation. Through these discussions determine if there is honest and free communication among all parties.

138. Build greater equity and reciprocity with the colleague (either a peer or mentee) by building a co-learning relationship.

As mentioned above, one of the important characteristics of an effective academic collaboration is honesty and cooperation. If the inherent power of collaborating individuals is not equal—whether based on position, tenure, reporting structures, etc.—it can become a significant difficulty. Co-learning is a beneficial way to frame collegial relationships that reduces power imbalance and/or competition. Co-learning emphasizes the valuable, varied skills and experiences that all individuals bring to collaborations. Especially when there is an imbalance in power or achievement (i.e., professor and student, pre-tenured and tenured faculty, etc.), co-learning creates an equitable dynamic in which everyone is contributing value. Benefits of addressing power issues include fewer conflict incidents, better communication, mutual collaboration, and motivation for completion.

139. As a team, set short-term and long-term goals for each project.

While many academics launch into collaborative projects without advanced planning, the establishment of general timelines from the beginning clarifies many potential questions. Therefore, develop a timeline that begins with the deadline for the submission and works backward to determine deadlines for significant phases of the project. By identifying both short-term and long-term goals, your team can enjoy the rewards of reaching goals mid-project rather than only at the conclusion. We all need to sustain positive energy in collaborations and lengthy projects; this strategy provides a means to energize your efforts through planning.

140. Develop mutually agreed upon assignment and deadlines for project responsibilities.

Identifying responsibilities greatly improves the quality of communication and efficiency of efforts. These designations do not have to be extensive, nor restrictive. Indeed, the participants must remember these tools support their work, instead of being ends in their own right. List the major responsibilities for the project in a three-column table format. One column lists the project responsibilities and the other two identify area headed by the name of each collaborator. You can then use a single check mark to denote who commits to the responsibility, and a second mark to indicate completion.

Working through developing these simple tools provides clear structure and deadlines for the project, and reveals many potential hidden assumptions or agendas. In some cases, people have difficulty reaching agreement at this point. It is invariably more helpful to unearth potential issues in the working relationship at the beginning of the project, rather than wasting several months of frustration. Develop and use the "chart of responsibilities" to negotiate tasks and facilitate your project management.

141. Cultivate trusting communication and confidence patterns in order to address concerns, barriers, or issues that will arise during your projects.

When beginning a new collaboration, determine how to communicate about difficult issues, what to do when your group cannot reach agreement, and the priority of trust and respect. These ground rules and values are cornerstones of effective working relationships. We are certain that you can think of a time when you felt attacked by a departmental conflict, manuscript rejection letter, or manuscript reviewer comments. Reflecting and discussing these experiences can help you learn how to address errors, academic disagreements, and misunderstandings without personal threat. For example, you might decide that if one person feels slighted by the other, that a face to face meeting (or phone or virtual, if distant meeting) will be scheduled within 48 hours.

The guidelines of your professional publication manual or code of ethics might be standards that you identify. Another strategy to consider is that if the collaborators cannot reach agreement, a mutually trusted colleague can serve as mediator. One needs to think about and address these issues early on, when everyone feels positive about the project and one another. Once communication difficulties begin, deciding upon conflict resolution strategies is obviously more complicated.

142. Establish protocols and other ways to be mutually accountable regarding the collaborative relationship.

When working on projects together, colleagues often need to be able to speak honestly and frankly with one another. Early in your project, discuss this need and how to approach it with each other. This practice establishes greater awareness of the issue, and guidance regarding future action. Usually, professionals know what habits or behaviors bother them, and how they work best. By learning each other's working styles and preferences, we have more opportunities to cultivate effective accountability without the emotional static of nagging, harassing, or blaming. Some academics may enjoy using the timetable and responsibility list as the focus point for discussions. Others might have prior experience that makes them using such formats less positive. Review the prior tip, regarding how to discuss difficult issues.

143. Discuss and determine routines and preferences for regular communication (weekly, bi-weekly, monthly) and organizing your work together.

There are several technology tools that can assist in accomplishing this tip. Creating your timeline in a shared virtual space and using it as a checklist allows transparency of the project's progress without having to email or phone another constantly. For instance, if you use Google Docs or Dropbox (Dropbox.com), any project partner can access the timeline 24 hours a day, 7 days a week to see the progress of the whole group. Other groups might prefer a hierarchical organizational system such as a shared online task organizer or a robust To-Do list.

The next level of sophistication is the project management platforms that have become popular since 2000. We suggest the online platforms tools, but encourage you to find one that meets your specific needs, does not absorb too much of your time, and with which all the members of your group feel comfortable. While many academics launch into collaborative projects without much planning, the establishment of timelines, communication choices, and charts of responsibilities greatly improves the quality and efficiency of efforts.

144. Determine mutually convenient meeting formats (i.e., in-person, phone, or virtual).

As mentioned above, using virtual technologies to support collaboration is beneficial and efficient. However, in our experience, in-person dialogue and planning cannot be rivaled for productivity and academic relationship building. For these reasons, we suggest that you determine how to meet in person prior to commencing the written project, even if your colleagues are distantly located (e.g., consider a conference or mid-point location as options).

Kathy has worked with many distant and international collaborators. Without fail the in-person meetings (at conferences or some other common location) provide much value in building these academic relationships. Having an initial planning meeting where you use many of the tips in this section is an excellent choice to cultivate a cooperative working relationship. As the project advances, you might not require meetings every week, day, or month; however, regularly scheduled project progress and troubleshooting will ensure greater accountability, formative assessment, communication, and overall progress. Consider the vast technology and in-person options for "meeting" and develop a mutually beneficial strategy.

145. Offer to provide feedback for one another on other academic projects.

You may offer to proofread or review occasional articles for one another, or provide a teaching observation. The time spent in working with another in different contexts may reveal new potential linkages or syntheses for future collaborations. Through these informal professional development activities, both participants stand to grow in understanding (new ideas and better practice for instance), build their portfolio (i.e., as an early academic you may list providing an observation for a colleague, and having a record of a peer observation in your CV), and strengthen your mutual understanding. Some authors in the literature refer to such colleagues as "critical friends." Among your critical friends you will likely discover professional relationships that may be long lasting and very rewarding.

146. Identify professional resources that will support the details of your project, such as writing tips, research methods, ethics, etc.

Together you and your collaborator/mentee can explore and discuss these resources. In the process, not only will you increase you individual and collective skills and perspective, but you will also build a better understanding and working relationship. Appendix A in this book has many such resources for your consideration and assistance. Your team might also consider campus or conference professional development to advance needed skills. The working relationship can include not only focus on academic outcomes, but also collaboration in professional growth.

147. Acknowledge milestones and celebrate successes together.

You will be working on each of your projects with your colleagues for at least several months. When you find a collaborator with whom you work well, be sure to demonstrate your appreciation with words and actions. One way to continue a good academic collaboration is to acknowledge milestones and celebrate successes. Certainly, at the completion of projects and when your work earns awards, you need to take time to celebrate the successes. However, we find that acknowledging milestones, congratulating each other, celebrating finishing the draft of your book or the uploading of the page proofs, and sharing these positive achievements builds positive relationships and good will. Whether they are by phone call, electronic greeting card, or victory email, those positive experiences help motivate us when the work seems like a long road.

Appendix A

Resources

Academic Life

Boice, Robert. 2000. *Advice for new faculty members*. New York, NY: Allyn & Bacon.

Colbeck, Carol L., Kerry Ann O'Meara, and Ann E. Austin. 2008. Educating integrated professionals: Theory and practice on preparation for the professoriate. San Francisco, CA: Jossey-Bass.

hooks, bell. 1994. *Teaching to transgress*. New York, NY: Routledge.

Miller, John P. 1994. *The contemplative practitioner*. Westport, CT: Bergin & Garvey.

Palmer, Parker J. 1999. *The courage to teach*. San Francisco, CA: Jossey Bass.

Palmer, Parker J. 1993. *To know as we are known: Education as a spiritual journey*. New York, NY: HarperCollins.

O'Reilley, Mary R. 1998. *Radical presence: Teaching as contemplative practice*. Portsmouth, NH: Boynton/Cook Publishers.

Schön, Donald. 1983. *The reflective practitioner*. New York, NY: Basic Books.

College Teaching

Adams, Mike, and Sally Brown. 2006. *Towards inclusive learning in higher education: Developing curricula for disabled students*. London, UK: Routledge.

Branche, Jerome, John W. Mullennix, and Ellen R. Cohn. 2007. *Diversity across the curriculum: A guide for faculty in higher education*. Bolton, MA: Anker Pub. Co.

Brookfield, Stephen B. 2009. *The skillful teacher: On technique, trust and responsiveness in the classroom*. (2nd ed.). San Francisco, CA: Jossey-Bass.

Burgstahler, Sharon. 2011b. Equal access: Universal Design of Instruction: A checklist for inclusive teaching. Retrieved from http://www.washington.edu/doit/Brochures/Academics/equal_access_udi.html

Burgstahler, Sharon. 2007. Applications of Universal Design in education. Seattle: University of Washington. Retrieved from http://www.washington.edu/doit/Brochures/PDF/app_ud_edu.pdf

Cranton, Patricia. 2001. *Becoming an authentic teacher in higher education*. Malabar, FL: Krieger Publishing.

Fink, L. Dee. 2003. *Creating significant learning experiences*. San Francisco, CA: Jossey-Bass.

Freire, Paulo. 1980. *Pedagogy of the oppressed*. New York, NY: Continuum.

Galbraith, Michael W. (ed). 2003. *Adult learning methods: A guide for effective instruction* (3rd ed). Malabar, FL: Krieger.

Lattuca, Lisa R., and Joan S. Stark. 2009. *Shaping the college curriculum: Academic plans in context*. San Francisco, CA: Jossey Bass.

Svinicki, Marilla D., and Wilbert J. McKeachie. 2011. *McKeachie's teaching tips: Strategies, research, and theory for college and university teachers*. Belmont, CA: Wadsworth, Cengage Learning.

Wlodkowski, Raymond, and Margery Ginsberg. 2010. *Diversity and motivation: Culturally responsive teaching* (2nd ed.). San Francisco, CA: Jossey Bass.

Dissertation and Literature Review

Bryant, Miles T. 2004. *The portable dissertation advisor*. Thousand Oaks, CA: Corwin Press.

Galvan, Jose. 2009. *Writing literature reviews: A guide for students of the social and behavioral sciences* (4th ed.). Glendale, CA: Pyrczak Publishing.

Hart, Chris. 1999. *Doing a literature review*. Thousand Oaks, CA: Sage.

Machi, Lawrence A., and Brenda T. McEvoy. 2007. *The literature review: Six steps to success*. Thousand Oaks, CA: Corwin Press.

Pyrczak, Fred. 2000. *Completing your thesis or dissertation: Professors share their techniques and strategies*. Glendale, CA: Pyrczak Publishing.

Pyrczak, Fred. 2008. *Evaluating research in academic journals* (4th ed.). Glendale, CA: Pyrczak Publishing.

Pyrczak, Fred, and Randall R. Bruce. 2010. *Writing empirical research reports*. (6th ed.). Glendale, CA: Pyrczak Publishing.

Roberts, Carol M. 2004. *The dissertation journey: A practical and comprehensive guide to planning, writing, and defending your dissertation*. Thousand Oaks, CA: Corwin Press.

Rudestam, Kjell Erik, and Rae R. Newton. 2007. *Surviving your dissertation: A comprehensive guide to content and process* (3rd ed). Thousand Oaks, CA: Sage.

Grant Funding Resources

COS. n.d. Pivot. Retrieved from http://pivot.cos.com/funding_main (Institutional subscription may be required, check with your organization.)

Foundation Center. n.d. The foundation grants index. New York, NY: Author. (Published annually).

Foundation Center. 2011. Foundation grants to individuals for 2011 (20th ed). New York, NY: Author. (Published annually).

Fulbright Foundation. 2011. Fulbright program. Retrieved from http://www.iie.org/fulbright

McDonough, Beverly, and Daniel Bazikian. 2011. *Annual register of grant support 2012: A directory of funding sources* (44th ed.). Medford, NJ: Information Today.

National Science Foundation. 2011. NSF grants. Retrieved from http://www.nsf.gov/

U.S. Department of Education. Grants database. Retrieved from http://www2.ed.gov/programs/find/title/index.html

U.S. Department of Health and Human Services. 2011. Interdisciplinary online grants database and submission system. Retrieved from http://www.grants.gov

U. S. Legislature. 2011. Federal register. Retrieved from http://www.gpo.gov/fdsys/

Grant Writing Resources

Barr, Margaret J., and George McClellan. 2011. *Budgets and financial management in higher education.* San Francisco, CA: Jossey Bass.

Barr, Margaret J. 2002. *Academic administrators guide to budgets and financial management.* San Francisco, CA: Jossey Bass.

Bauer, David G. 2011. *The 'how to' grants manual: Successful grantseeking techniques for obtaining public and private grants.* (7th ed). New York, NY: Rowman & Littlefield.

Carlson, Mim, and Tori O'Neil-McElrath. 2008. *Winning grants step by step.* San Francisco, CA: Jossey-Bass.

Henson, Kenneth T. 2008. *Grant writing in higher education.* New York, NY: Allyn Bacon.

The Foundation Center. 2011. Guide to funding research. Retrieved from http://www.foundationcenter.org/getstarted/tutorials/gfr/begin.html

Karsh, Ellen, and Arlen Sue Fox. 2009. *The only grant-writing book you'll ever need: Top grant writers and grant givers share their secrets* (3rd ed.). New York, NY: Basic Books.

National Institute of Health. 2011. NIH/AID Guide for proposal writing. Retrieved from http://www.niaid.nih.gov/researchfunding/grant/pages/aag.aspx

NSF. 2011. NSF Guide to proposal writing. Retrieved from http://www.nsf.gov/pubs/2004/nsf04016/nsf04016_1.htm

Technology and Teaching

Conceicao, Simone C. O., and Rosemary M. Lehman. 2011. *Managing online instructor workload: Strategies for finding balance and success.* San Francisco, CA: Jossey-Bass.

Conrad, Rita-Marie, and J. Ana Donaldson. 2004. *Engaging the online learner.* San Francisco, CA: Jossey-Bass.

Jonassen, David H., Jane Howland, Joi Moore, and Rose M. Marra. 2003. *Learning to solve problems with technology* (2nd ed.). Upper Saddle River, NJ: Merrill Prentice Hall.

King, Kathleen P., and Thomas Cox. (Eds). 2011. *The professor's guide to taming technology: Leveraging digital media, Web 2.0 and more for learning.* Series: Innovative perspectives of higher education: research, theory and practice. Charlotte, NC: Information Age Publishing.

King, Kathleen P. and Joan K. Griggs. (Eds.). 2007. *Harnessing innovative technologies in higher education: Access, equity, policy, and instruction.* Madison, WI: Atwood Publishing.

Palloff, Rena M., and Keith Pratt. 2007. *Building online learning communities: Effective strategies for the virtual classroom* (2nd ed.). San Francisco, CA: Jossey-Bass.

Research Resources

Chang, Heewon. 2008. *Autoethnography as method.* Walnut Creek, CA: Left Coast Press.

Creswell, John W. 2008. *Research design: Quantitative, qualitative and mixed methods.* (3rd ed.). Thousand Oaks, CA: Sage.

Ellis, Carolyn. 2004. *The ethnographic I.* New York, NY: Altamira Press.

Fowler, Floyd J. 1995. *Improving survey questions.* Thousand Oaks, CA: Sage.

Fowler, Floyd J. 2008. *Survey research methods.* (4th ed). Thousand Oaks, CA: Sage.

Gall, Meredith D., Walter R. Borg, and Joyce P. Gall. 1996. *Educational research: An introduction* (6th ed.). White Plains, NY: Longman.

Glaser, Barney G., and Anslem L. Strauss. 1967. *The discovery of grounded theory: Strategies for qualitative research.* Chicago, IL: Aldine.

Greene, Jennifer C. 2007. *Mixed methods in social inquiry.* Thousand Oaks, CA: Sage.

Johnson, Burke, and Larry B. Christensen. 2010. *Educational research: Quantitative, qualitative and mixed approaches.* (4th ed.) Thousand Oaks, CA: Sage.

Merriam, Sharan B. 2009. *Qualitative research: A guide to design and implementation.* San Francisco, CA: Jossey-Bass.

Miles, Matthew B., and Michael Huberman. 1994. *Qualitative data analysis: An expanded sourcebook* (2nd) ed. Thousand Oaks, CA: Corwin Press.

Plano Clark, Vicki L., and John W. Creswell. 2008. *The mixed methods reader.* Thousand Oaks, CA: Sage.

Seidman, Irving. 2006. *Interviewing as qualitative research: A guide for researchers in education and the social sciences.* New York, NY: Teachers College Press.

Teddlie, Charles B., and Abbas Tashakkori. 2008. *Foundations of mixed methods research: Integrating quantitative and qualitative approaches in the social and behavioral sciences*. Thousand Oaks, CA: Sage.

Treiman, Donald J. 2009. *Quantitative data analysis: Doing social research to test ideas*. San Francisco, CA: Jossey Bass.

Yin, Robert K. 2008. *Case study research: Design and methods*. Thousand Oaks, CA: Sage.

Writing Resources

Boice, Robert. 1990. *Professors as writers: A self-help guide to productive writing*. Norman, OK: New Forums Press.

Elbow, Peter. 1973. *Writing without teachers*. New York, NY: Oxford University Press.

Goldberg, Natalie. 2005. *Writing down the bones: Freeing the writer within*. Boston, MA: Shambalah.

Lamott, Anne. 1995. *Bird by bird: Some instructions on writing and life*. New York, NY: Anchor.

Machi, Lawrence A., and Brenda T. McEvoy. 2008. *The literature review: Six steps to success*. Thousand Oaks, CA: Corwin Press.

Moore, Dinty W. 2012. *The mindful writer: Noble truths of the writing life*. Boston, MA: Wisdom Publications.

Rocco, Tonnette S., and Tim Hatcher. 2010. *The handbook of scholarly writing and publishing*. San Francisco, CA: Jossey Bass.

Strunk, William, and E. B. White. 1999. *The elements of style* (4th ed.) New York, NY: Longman. (Note: Readers, find the 105 pp version [4th ed]; there are condensed versions published!)

Wolfe, Joanna. 2010. *Team writing: A guide to working in groups*. Bedford, MA: St. Martin's Press.

Appendix B

Research and Publication Tracking Tables

Gantt Chart for research and publication projects

	20___												20___					
	JAN	FEB	MAR	APR	MAY	JUNE	JULY	AUG	SEPT	OCT	NOV	DEC	JAN	FEB	MAR	APR	MAY	JUNE
Research Project #1																		
Research method determined																		
Participants																		
Literature review																		
IRB SUBMIT – APPROVE																		
Data																		
Analysis																		
Outline																		
Write draft																		
Final version																		
Final refs																		
Proofed by colleagues																		
Cover letter																		
Submitted																		
Journal 1 identity																		
Journal 2																		
Journal 3																		
IN PRESS																		
Published – date and details																		

Gantt Chart for research and publication projects

	20___												20___					
	JAN	FEB	MAR	APR	MAY	JUNE	JULY	AUG	SEPT	OCT	NOV	DEC	JAN	FEB	MAR	APR	MAY	JUNE
Research Project #2																		
Research method determined																		
Participants																		
Literature review																		
IRB SUBMIT – APPROVE																		
Data																		
Analysis																		
Outline																		
Write draft																		
Final version																		
Final refs																		
Proofed by colleagues																		
Cover letter																		
Submitted																		
Journal 1 Identity																		
Journal 2																		
Journal 3																		
IN PRESS																		
Published – date and details																		

Gantt Chart for research and publication projects (© 2010, Kathleen P. King)

EXAMPLE COMPLETED: Gantt Chart for research and publication projects																		
	2014												2015					
	JAN	FEB	MAR	APR	MAY	JUNE	JULY	AUG	SEPT	OCT	NOV	DEC	JAN	FEB	MAR	APR	MAY	JUNE
Research Project: Social Media & Financial Literacy																		
Research method determined	XXXXXX	XXXXXX																
Participants		XXX	XX															
Literature review			XXX	XXXX														
IRB SUBMIT – APPROVE				XXXX														
Data				XXXX	XX													
Analysis					XXXXXX	XXXX												
Outline							XXXX											
Write draft							XXX											
Final version								XXXXXX										
Final refs								XX										
Proofed by colleagues									Sept 1 2014									
Cover letter																		
Submitted													Jan1 2015?					
Journal 1 Identity	LLL																	
Journal 2	CT																	
Journal 3	SCJ																	
IN PRESS																		
Published – date and details																		

Completed example of Gantt Chart for research and publication projects (© 2010, Kathleen P. King)

EXAMPLE COMPLETED: Gantt Chart for research and publication projects

	2014												2015					
	JAN	FEB	MAR	APR	MAY	JUNE	JULY	AUG	SEPT	OCT	NOV	DEC	JAN	FEB	MAR	APR	MAY	JUNE
Research Project: International Study of Women Leaders in Higher Education																		
Research method determined	XXXXXX																	
Participants		XXXXXX	XXXXXX															
Literature review				XXXXXX														
IRB SUBMIT – APPROVE					XXXXXX													
Data						XXXXXX												
Analysis							XXXXXX	XXXXXX										
Outline									XXXXXX	XXXXXX								
Write draft										XXXXXX								
Final version											xx							
Final refs												Dec 1 2014						
Proofed by colleagues																		
Cover letter																		
Submitted															Mar 1 2015			
Journal 1 Identity	JFD																	
Journal 2	IJDF																	
Journal 3	LLL																	
IN PRESS																		
Published – date and details																		

RESEARCH AND SUBMISSION TRACKING														
Professor Name Here														
Currently Being Researched														
Name of project	Res method	Data	Analysis	Outline	Written	Refs	Proofed–KPK team	Proofed–DS	Cover letter	Submitted	Journal 1	Journal 2	Journal 3	Editor's email address
1														
2														
Writing in Progress														
Name of project	Res method	Data	Analysis	Outline	Written	Refs	Proofed–KPK team	Proofed–DS	Cover letter	Submitted	Journal 1	Journal 2	Journal 3	Editor's email address
1														
2														
Submitted to Journal: Waiting														
Name of project	Res method	Data	Analysis	Outline	Written	Refs	Proofed–KPK team	Proofed–DS	Cover letter	Submitted	Journal 1	Journal 2	Journal 3	Editor's email address
1														
2														
Accepted: In Press (move to CV!)														
Name of project	Res method	Data	Analysis	Outline	Written	Refs	Proofed–KPK team	Proofed–DS	Cover letter	Submitted	Journal 1	Journal 2	Journal 3	Editor's email address
1														
2														
3														

Research and submission tracking (© 2009, Kathleen P. King)

References

Apps, Jerold. 1991. *Mastering the teaching of adults*. Malabar, FL: Krieger.

Beecher, Henry K. 1966. Laying ethical foundations for informed consent. *New England Journal of Medicine* 274 (24) June: 1374–1360.

Boyer, Ernest. 1997. *Scholarship reconsidered*. San Francisco, CA: Jossey-Bass.

Burgstahler, Sharon. 2011a. Universal Design of Instruction: Definition, principles, guidelines, and examples. Retrieved from http://www.washington.edu/doit/Brochures/Academics/instruction.html

Burgstahler, Sharon. 2011b. Equal access: Universal Design of Instruction: A checklist for inclusive teaching. Retrieved from http://www.washington.edu/doit/Brochures/Academics/equal_access_udi.html

Burgstahler, Sharon, and Rebecca C. Cory. 2008. *Universal design in higher education: From principles to practice*. Cambridge, MA: Harvard Educational Press.

Buzan, Tony. 1999. *The mind map book: Radiant thinking*. London, England: BBC Books.

Covey, Stephen. 2004. *Seven habits of highly effective people*. New York, NY: Free Press.

Cranton, Patricia. 2001. *Becoming an authentic teacher in higher education*. Malabar, FL: Krieger Publishing.

Donald, Janet. 2003. *Learning to think: Disciplinary perspectives*. San Francisco, CA: Jossey-Bass.

Fink, L. Dee. 2003. *Creating significant learning experiences*. San Francisco, CA: Jossey-Bass.

Goldberg, Natalie. 2005. *Writing down the bones: Freeing the writer within*. Boston, MA: Shambalah.

Hamilton, Jon. 2008. Think you're multitasking? Think again. National Public Radio. Retrieved Oct 2, 2008, from http://www.npr.org/templates/story/story.php?storyId=95256794

King, Kathleen P. 2011. Revelations of adaptive technology hiding in your operating system. In *The professor's guide to taming technology: Leveraging digital media, Web 2.0 and more for learning,* edited by Kathleen P. King and Thomas Cox. Series: Innovative perspectives of higher education: Research, theory and practice (183-200). Charlotte, NC: Information Age Publishing, Inc.

King, Kathleen P., and Thomas Cox, eds. 2011. *The professor's guide to taming technology: Leveraging digital media, Web 2.0 and more for learning*. Series: Innovative perspectives of higher education: research, theory and practice. Charlotte, NC: Information Age Publishing.

Miller, John P. 1994. *The contemplative practitioner*. Westport, CT: Bergin & Garvey.

Moore, Dinty W. 2012. *The mindful writer: Noble truths of the writing life*. Boston, MA: Wisdom Publications.

O'Reilley, Mary R. 1998. *Radical presence*. San Francisco, CA: Jossey-Bass.

Palmer, Parker J. 1999. *The courage to teach*. San Francisco, CA: Jossey Bass.

Rico, Gabriele. 1983. *Writing the natural way*. New York: Penguin Books.

Rubinstein, Joshua S., David E. Meyer, and Jeffrey E. Evans. 2001. Executive control of cognitive processes in task switching. *Journal of Experimental Psychology: Human Perception and Performance* 27 (4) Aug: 763-797.

Schön, Donald. 1983. *The reflective practitioner*. New York: Basic Books.

Schrecker, Ellen. 2010. *The lost soul of higher education*. New York: The New Press.

Scott, Sally, Joan McGuire, and Stan Shaw. 2001. *Principles of Universal Design for Instruction*. Storrs, CT: University of Connecticut, Center on Postsecondary Education and Disability.

Index

About the Authors

Kathleen P. King, Ed.D., is a department chair and professor of Adult, Career, and Higher Education at the University of South Florida, Tampa. She is also co-editor of an international journal and series editor for three book series with Information Age Publishing. She enjoys walking the academic journey with doctoral students and candidates, and stays vitally connected to everyday needs of faculty as a certified faculty and life coach by assisting them in advancing their careers. King's major areas of research and keynote speaking include distance learning, higher education, transformative learning, professional development, diversity issues, and instructional technology. She is the author/editor of 21 books and over 165 published articles and research papers.

King's recent recognitions include induction into the International Continuing and Adult Education Hall of Fame (ICAE) in 2011, and the AERA Outstanding Research Publication in 2009. Her continuing international research spans China, France, and Canada. She frequently keynotes and presents refereed research and presentations at educational and interdisciplinary academic conferences. Prior to joining the USF faculty in 2010, for 13 years Dr. King was at Fordham University in New York City as a professor, program director, and university administrator. Dr. King earned her Ed.D. and M.Ed. in Higher and Adult Education from Widener University, Chester, PA.

Dr. ***Ann Cranston-Gingras*** is a professor of special education, department chair, and director of the Center for Migrant Education at the University of South Florida, Tampa. She has been the Principal Investigator and Director of many externally funded projects including currently funded federal grants serving students from migrant farm worker families. She also has been instrumental in helping to secure private funds to support students from migrant backgrounds who are preparing to become teachers and educational leaders. Her research focuses on the educational needs of youth who have been marginalized by schools and society, including students with disabilities and those from migrant farm worker backgrounds.

Cranston-Gingras' is the author or co-author of numerous book chapters and refereed journal articles and is the co-author of the text, *Teaching Learners with Diverse Abilities*, and co-editor of the book, *Rethinking Professional Issues in Special Education*. She teaches undergraduate and graduate classes in special education and supervises doctoral students. She has mentored over twenty doctoral students through completion of their dissertation research. Dr. Cranston-Gingras' recent recognitions include The Hispanic Heritage Society's Pathways and Amiga awards, The Florida Department of Education Migrant Program Administrator of the Year Award, The University of South Florida Latino Association Faculty Award and the University of South Florida President's Award for Faculty Excellence.